DO-IT-YOURSELF JAPANESE THROUGH COMICS

DO-IT-YOURSELF JAPANESE
THROUGH COMICS

KAZUHIKO NAGATOMO
MIHO STEINBERG

KODANSHA INTERNATIONAL
Tokyo · New York · London

DO-IT-YOURSELF JAPANESE THROUGH COMICS is based upon "Kiso Kosu: Basic Japanese," which was originally serialized in *The Nihongo Journal* (published by ALC Press Inc.) between April 1993 and March 1994.

Distributed in the United States by Kodansha America, Inc., 114, Fifth Avenue, New York, New York 10011, and in the United Kingdom and continental Europe by Kodansha Europe Ltd., 95 Aldwych, London WC2CB 4JF. Published by Kodansha International Ltd., 17-14, Otowa 1-chome, Bunkyo-ku, Tokyo 112 and Kodansha America Inc.

Text copyright © 1995 by Kazuhiko Nagatomo and Miho Steinberg
Illustrations copyright © 1995 by Yoshiyuki Asano
Designed by Katsui Design Office Inc.
Edited by guild
All rights reserved. No part of this publication may be reproduced in any form or by any means without prior written permission of the publishers.

First edition, 1995
95 96 97 98 10 9 8 7 6 5 4 3 2 1

ISBN 4 - 7700 - 1935 - 1

Printed in Japan by Dai-Nippon Printing Company

Library of Congress cataloging in publication data available

CONTENTS

	How to use this book: For students	7
	How to use this book: For Japanese language teachers	8
1. はじめまして	How do you do?	10
2. すみません	I am sorry.	18
3. どうぞ おだいじに	Please take care of yourself.	26
4. ありがとう ございます	Thank you.	34
5. かんぱい	Cheers!	42
6. もしもし	Hello.	50
7. ごしゅうしょうさまです	You have my sympathies.	58
8. どちらまで	Where to?	66
9. これ どうぞ	This is for you.	74
10. 今年も どうぞ よろしく	I look forward to our continued relationship over this year.	82
11. お世話に なります	Thank you in advance.	90
12. がんばって ください	Hang in there.	98
	Answers	107
	Grammar Index	110

HOW TO USE THIS BOOK FOR STUDENTS

Designed so that students can learn Japanese the fun way, either alone or in a group, DO-IT-YOURSELF JAPANESE THROUGH COMICS is aimed at beginners familiar with hiragana, katakana, numbers, and some simple expressions.

The book comprises twelve modules, each divided into six sections: Dialogue (using cartoon strips,) Culture, Pronunciation, Notes, Drills, and Tasks. Since the level of grammar and vocabulary is consistent throughout, the student may start from any module.

Dialogue

This section introduces a variety of handy and natural expressions used in everyday conversation. We suggest that the student use the comic strip to practice these expressions until he or she is able to reproduce them without further reference to the dialogue. For more effective language learning, listen repeatedly to the same dialogue on the cassette tape (available separately from good book stores or directly from the publisher.) Alternatively group members can take on roles and act out the comic strip.

Culture

A brief article outlining a Japanese custom, or lifestyle aspect, related to the main topic of each module enables the student to compare the Japanese way of life with his or her own and fosters a deeper understanding of Japanese society and culture.

Pronunciation

Dialogue is presented entirely in romaji using a variation of the Hepburn system. The student should repeatedly read aloud while paying attention to stress and the signs marking pitch. In order to perfect one's grasp of the characteristics of Japanese pronunciation, the student should listen to the tape and try to reproduce what he or she hears.

Notes

These are concise explanations of the meaning, general usage, and grammar of sentences that appear in each module. The student should refer to the notes each time he or she learns a sentence. The note numbers (marked with a square) correspond to the numbers in the comic strip.

Drills

Drill 1 comprises practice questions relating to the dialogue, while Drill 2 relates to notes. When attempting the Drills, the student can refer to the Dialogue and Note sections and, if necessary, to the answers at the back of the book.

Tasks

A diverse selection of wordgame-based activities that can be tackled individually or in a group. All vocabulary appears in the word list at the bottom of the page or somewhere in the same module.

HOW TO USE THIS BOOK — FOR JAPANESE LANGUAGE TEACHERS

This self-study teaching aid is aimed at beginners who have completed approximately thirty hours of Japanese language study and have mastered hiragana, katakana, and various simple expressions. However, this book's usage of manga and its emphasis on Japanese culture make it an enjoyable and unique learning tool suitable for classroom or individual teaching.

DO-IT-YOURSELF JAPANESE THROUGH COMICS is not a grammar-based book, nor does the level of difficulty increase progressively throughout the book. Consequently, study can begin from any module and the order of study be determined by student interest or class requirements.

Dialogue

It is a good idea to familiarize the students with the manga dialogue by having them listen repeatedly to the cassette tape (available separately from good book stores.) When the students have a grasp of the conversation, the teacher can organize related activities, such as mixing up the cartoon frames and getting the students to put them together again in the correct order, or eliminating the words and supplying the students with the relevant Notes and other explanations so that they can recreate the section using the pictures.

Culture

The teacher should make full use of the culture section, since it helps rouse student interest when beginning a module and encourages understanding of the cultural topic forming the backdrops for the dialogue.

Pronunciation

The teacher should instruct the students in pitch and stress by having them listen to the tape several times and repeating the contents aloud. With this method the students ought to acquire the characteristics of Japanese pronunciation, such as unvoiced vowels. Another good way to teach pronunciation is to get the students to take roles and act out the sentences in the dialogue, or improvise and develop conversations.

Notes

The aim of the notes on usage and grammar is to give students a grasp of the contents of the dialogue in as short and concise a form as possible. The notes do not include detailed grammatical explanations for each sentence. However, the teacher may add related sample sentences or extra explanations according to the competence of the student.

Drills

We recommend that the teacher continue drill practice until the students fully understand the dialogue. In the classroom, in particular, teachers should make sure the students get enough practice by introducing similar or new drills.

Tasks

The teacher should be sure to spend plenty of time on this section, answering any questions from the students.
When going through the Drills or Tasks in the classroom, the teacher may want to liven up the lesson by hiding the word lists.

HOW TO USE THIS BOOK   DRAMATIS PERSONAE

Mary Smith

Mary Smith is a young American woman from Denver, Colorado. Her interest in Japan began when she met Tatsuhiko Sato at a friend's party in the US. Since then she has been determined to learn Japanese and work in Japan.

Guo Fu Lin

After arriving in Japan a year ago, Guo Fu has managed to find work with an automobile manufacturer that is trying to expand business is China. It was through his job that he met Tatsuhiko Sato who introduced him to a set of new friends.

Tatsuhiko Sato

After a busy day at office, Tatsuhiko Sato likes to relax by teaching Japanese to his foreign friends. As he works for a trading company that does business all over the world, he has many oppotunities to meet people from different cultures.

Akiko Sato

Akiko has been married to Tatsuhiko for over twenty years. Until recently she taught English at a small private junior high school, but had to quit so that she could look after her elderly in-laws.

Songhui Kim

A hard-working and dedicated college student, Songhui came to Japan about six months ago to study Japanese culture. Since Tatsuhiko Sato is an old friend of her father, she often spends time with the Sato family.

Masatoshi Suzuki

Professor Suzuki is a renowned scholar of Japanese Buddhist art who teaches Songhui at college. When he's not giving lectures, he can be found pottering around small Buddhist temples with his granddaughter, Aiko.

A word on imitative and onomatopoeic words in Japanese comics

Just like American comics, Japanese cartoon strips or manga use imitative and onomatopoeic words like "bang" and "zzzz." Most of these words appear in katakana script, but can also be written with hiragana. You will find that this book also uses many imitative and onomatopoeic words. The beginner need not make a special effort to learn and use them, since many have different meanings for different situations, and quite a few are only used in manga. Nevertheless, such words appear in the word list marked with a circle (○) so that the student may understand the content and nuance of the cartoon. In some cases an English translation or explanation of the context is included: as long as the student understands this, it is not necessary to commit the words to memory.

1 はじめまして　　How do you do?

DIALOGUE

VOCABULARY

- 名古屋 Nagoya
- 佐藤さん Mr. Sato
- 林さん Mr. Lin
- に to
- スミスさん Ms. Smith
- 紹介する to introduce
- メアリ・スミス Mary Smith
- です am, is, are
- どうぞ よろしく おねがいします Nice to meet you
- 林国福 Lin Guo Fu
- はじめまして How do you do?
- お国 country
- どちら where
- アメリカ America
- きのう yesterday
- 来ました came
- グォーツ sound of jet engine
- そうですか Is that so?

OBJECTIVES:
Introducing yourself, using polite Japanese and asking simple questions.

- わたし I
- 1年前に one year ago
- 中国 China
- から from
- ギャッ cry of surprise
- アハハ、ハハハ、ホホ sound of laughter
- ツーッ sound-effect word of a falling spider

CULTURE

Meishi

Widespread use of *meishi* helps to keep introductions brief and to the point in Japan. Providing essential information about affiliation and position in an organization, such as a college or company, these indispensable business cards can be ordered inexpensively and promptly from the local printer. With or without a *meishi*, however, it is still recommended to introduce yourself with an explanation of where you work or study. Typical examples include, "Hello, I'm Hiroe Tomizawa, a sophomore at Osaka University." Or "My name is Kenta Watanabe and I'm the production manager at Toyoda Autos." Remember, too, that a bow or *ojigi* is preferred to a handshake in Japan.

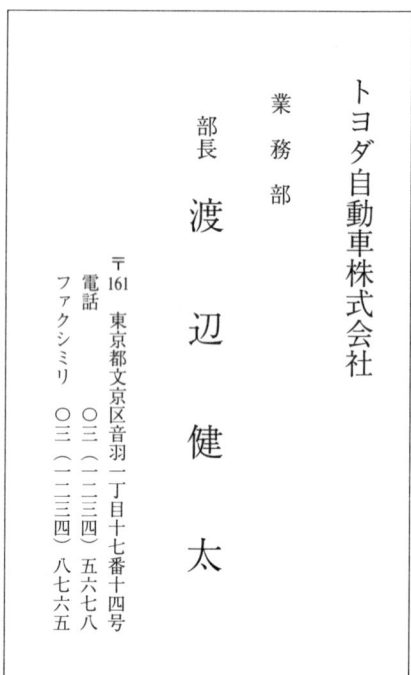

PRONUNCIATION

Listen to the tape and repeat. High pitches are marked with ⌈ and low pitches with ⌉. All words appearing in **bold** should be stressed. Note that hyphenated phrases are treated as one word.

1. Satoo-san-ga Rin-san-ni **Sumisu-san**-o shookai-suru.

2. Rin-san, **Sumisu-san**-o go-shookai-shimasu.

3. Meari-Sumisu-desu. Doozo **yoroshiku** onegai-shimasu.

4. Rin-Kokufuku-desu. Hajimemashite. Doozo **yoroshiku**.

5. **O-kuni**-wa dochira-desu-ka.

6. Amerika-desu. **Kinoo** Nagoya-e kimashita.

7. Soo-desu-ka. Watashi-wa **ichi-nen-mae**-ni Chuugoku-kara kimashita.

NOTES

1 佐藤さんが 林さんに スミスさんを 紹介する。
Mr. Sato introduces Ms. Smith to Mr. Lin.

❶ The first sentence follows the basic structure:

| subject | が | indirect object | に | direct object | を | verb |

❷ が is a particle used to show the subject of a verb.

❸ に is another particle, used here to show the indirect object of the same verb.

❹ を, also a particle, marks the direct object of the verb.

佐藤さん[subject] が 林さん[indirect object] に スミスさん[direct object] を 紹介する[verb]。

❺ Note that the topic of the sentence takes the particle は.

鈴木先生[(subject) topic] は 学生[indirect object] に 数学[direct object] を 教える[verb]。
Professor Suzuki teaches mathematics to his students.

学生に[(indirect object) topic] は 鈴木先生[subject] が 数学[direct object] を 教える[verb]。

数学[(direct object) topic] は 鈴木先生[subject] が 学生[indirect object] に 教える[verb]。

2 林さん、スミスさんを ご紹介します。
Mr. Lin, allow me to introduce Ms. Smith to you.

In this sentence the verb 紹介する is in the polite form. The polite form or です／ます form of a Japanese predicate is used to show respect to a listener. Accordingly, it is better to use this form when addressing superiors such as a boss or teacher, and when talking to people whom you don't know very well. Conversely, the plain form or dictionary form of a verb is used in conversations between friends.

polite form	plain form
紹介します (to introduce)	紹介する
来ました (came)	来た
アメリカです (is America)	アメリカだ

3 メアリ・スミスです。どうぞ よろしく おねがいします。
Hello, my name is Mary Smith. I'm very pleased to meet you.

❶ です is the polite form of the so-called copula. A copula is used to link two nouns or a noun and an adjective in a sentence where no obvious verb can be used. Here, the first noun わたし(I) has been omitted because, from the context, it is clear enough who Mary Smith might be. In English, the verb "to be" is very often used like a copula.

❷ どうぞ よろしく おねがいします。 This expression is often used when introducing yourself and other times when asking a vague kind of favor of someone. There is no precise English equivalent, but in a similar situation, one might say "nice to meet you" or words to that effect.

4 林国福です。はじめまして。どうぞ よろしく。
I'm Lin Guo Fu. How do you do?

はじめまして is also used when introducing yourself. Again, there is no direct equivalent in English, but it is used rather like "how do you do?"

5 お国は どちらですか。
Where do you come from?

❶ お is a prefix used to make the so-called honorific form of nouns. In many instances, it has now lost any sense of attaching honor to the person being addressed, but お国 is still a useful word, indicating, as above, "your country."

❷ どちら is a less direct and therefore more polite way of asking どこ or "where?"

❸ か is a particle that usually comes at the end of sentences, and functions in a similar way to a question mark in English.

6 アメリカです。きのう 名古屋へ 来ました。
I come from the United States. I arrived in Nagoya yesterday.

❶ The particle へ indicates where someone or something is going or coming. In the above sentence, the place where Mary Smith began her journey has been left out. We can assume, from the dialogue, that it was America, and if it had been included, it would have been followed by the particle から which indicates where someone or something came from.

❷ Any part of a sentence that is understood by both the speaker and the listener is considered redundant and can often be deleted in Japanese. E.g. 日本へ(to Japan) has been omitted from **7** since this is easily understood from the context.

❸ 来ました(came) is the past tense of 来ます. You just change ます into ました to form the past tense. Similary, as in Drills and Tasks, 紹介する→紹介しました(introduced), 行きます→行きました(went), 帰ります→帰りました(returned).

7 そうですか。わたしは 1年前に 中国から 来ました。
Really? I came over from China a year ago.

❶ そうですか This common phrase is used when a listener wants to register that he has heard and understood what the speaker has just said. English equivalents include "Is that right?" and "Really?"

❷ Here, に is used to show when something took place, rather like the prepositions, "on" and "at."

❸ から tells us where Lin came from.

DRILLS

1. 質問に 答えなさい。
Answer the following questions.

1 佐藤さんは だれを 紹介しましたか。→ (　　　　　)を 紹介しました。

2 だれに 紹介しましたか。→ (　　　　　)に 紹介しました。

3 だれが 中国から 来ましたか。→ (　　　　　)です。

4 きのう だれが 名古屋へ 来ましたか。→ (　　　　　)です。

2. 次の 国は 地図の 中の どの 国ですか。番号で 答えなさい。
Match the countries listed below to the numbered locations on the world map.

a メキシコ　　b ロシア　　c タイ　　d エジプト　　e アルゼンチン
f イギリス　　g アメリカ　　h モンゴル　　i インド　　j フィンランド
k カナダ　　l フランス　　m ブラジル　　n イラン　　o オーストラリア

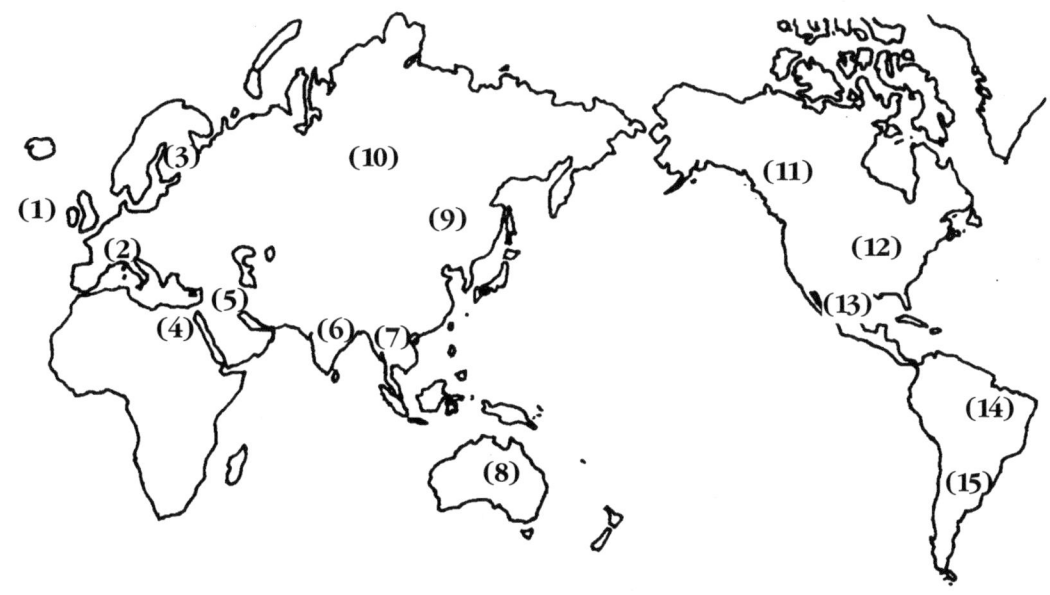

VOCABULARY

- だれ who
- 紹介(しょうかい)しました introduced
- メキシコ Mexico
- ロシア Russia
- タイ Thailand
- エジプト Egypt
- アルゼンチン Argentina
- イギリス England
- アメリカ America
- モンゴル Mongolia
- インド India
- フィンランド Finland
- カナダ Canada
- フランス France
- ブラジル Brazil
- イラン Iran
- オーストラリア Australia

TASKS

1. みんなは どこから 来たか。
Where did they all come from?

4月17日(土曜日)の 午後 2時に みんなが 佐藤さんの うちへ 来ました。みんなは どこから 来ましたか。下の スケジュールを 見て、答えなさい。

Everyone visited Mr. Sato's house at 2:00 P.M. on Saturday, April 17. But where were they immediately before 2:00 P.M.? Use the schedule below to help you fill in the blanks.

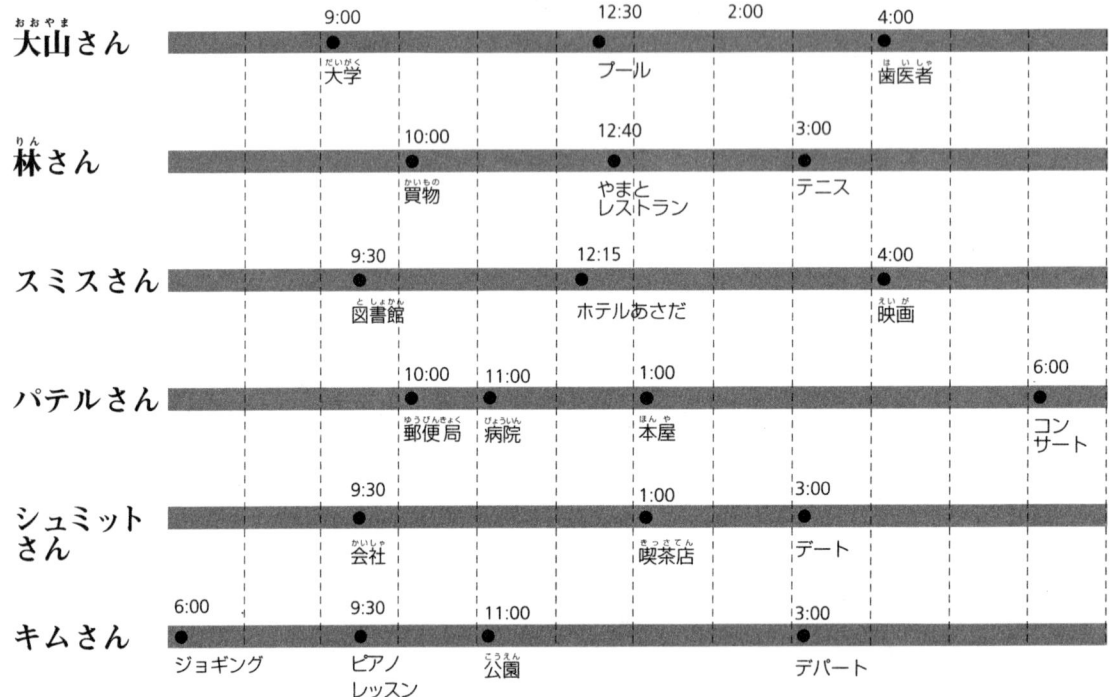

大山さんは (**1**　　　) から、林さんは (**2**　　　) から、スミスさんは (**3**　　　) から、パテルさんは (**4**　　　) から、シュミットさんは (**5**　　　) から、キムさんは (**6**　　　) から 佐藤さんの うちへ 来ました。

VOCABULARY

- 4月 (しがつ) April
- 17日 (じゅうしちにち) 17th
- 土曜日 (どようび) Saturday
- の of
- 午後 (ごご) P.M., in the afternoon
- 2時 (にじ) 2 o'clock
- に at
- みんな all, everyone
- うち home, house
- へ to
- どこ where
- から from
- 下 (した) below
- スケジュール schedule
- 見 (み) て looking at
- 答 (こた) えなさい answer: an imperative form
- 大学 (だいがく) college
- プール swimming pool
- 歯医者 (はいしゃ) dentist
- 買物 (かいもの) shopping
- やまとレストラン Yamato Restaurant
- テニス tennis
- 図書館 (としょかん) library
- ホテルあさだ Hotel Asada
- 映画 (えいが) movie
- 郵便局 (ゆうびんきょく) post office
- 病院 (びょういん) hospital
- 本屋 (ほんや) bookstore
- コンサート concert
- 会社 (かいしゃ) company
- 喫茶店 (きっさてん) coffee shop
- デート date
- ジョギング jogging
- ピアノレッスン piano lesson
- 公園 (こうえん) park
- デパート department store

2. 佐藤さんの 旅行コース
Mr. Sato's grand tour

佐藤さんは 去年 ヨーロッパへ 行きました。

佐藤さんの 旅行コースは A、B、C、D の どれでしょう。

Last year, Mr. Sato made a grand tour of Europe. The following clues will help you work out which route he took on his trip.

1. 佐藤さんは オスロ (Oslo)、ヘルシンキ (Helsinki)、ロンドン (London)、パリ (Paris)、リスボン (Lisbon)、ベルリン (Berlin)、ローマ (Rome)、アテネ (Athens)へ 行きました。
2. 東京から ローマへ 行きました。
3. そこから リスボンへ 行きました。
4. パリへ 行く 前に、ロンドンへ 行きました。
5. パリから オスロへ 行って、すぐ パリへ 帰りました。
6. パリから ベルリンへ 行って、そこから ヘルシンキへ 行きました。
7. ヘルシンキから ローマへ 行く 前に、アテネへ 行きました。
8. ローマから 東京へ 帰りました。

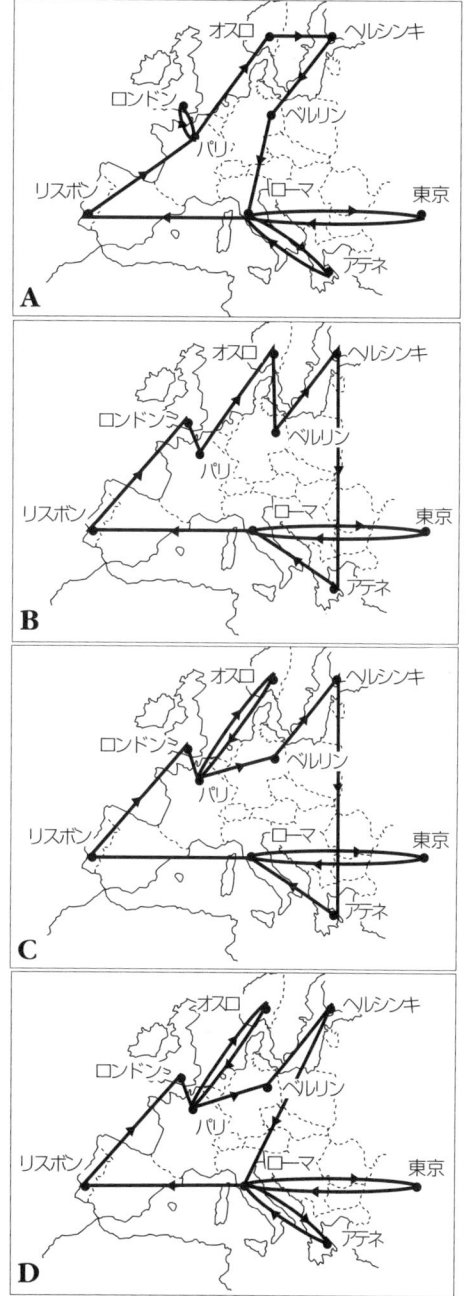

VOCABULARY

- 去年 (きょねん) last year
- ヨーロッパ Europe
- 行 (い) きました went
- 旅行 (りょこう) コース traveling itinerary
- どれ which
- でしょう will probably be
- そこ there, that place
- パリへ行く前 (まえ) に before [one] goes/went to Paris
- すぐ soon, right away
- 行 (い) って going
- 帰 (かえ) りました went/came back, returned

NOTES

パリへ 行く 前に ロンドンへ 行きました
Note that although this is a formal sentence, only the main verb needs to be in the polite form. As パリへ 行く 前に is a subordinate clause, the verb remains in the plain form. Remember you only have to be polite at the end of the sentence in Japanese.

2 すみません   I am sorry.

DIALOGUE

1. スミスさんが スピード違反で 警察に つかまった。スミスさんの 運転免許証は 国際免許証だ。

2. 運転免許証を 見せて ください。

3. はい、ここに あります。国際免許証 です。

4. 番号は これですね。ここは 40キロ以下で 走る ところです。60キロは いけません。

はい。すみません。

VOCABULARY

- スミスさん Ms. Smith
- スピード違反で due to speeding violation
- 警察に by the police
- つかまった was caught
- の of
- 運転免許証 driver's license
- は as for, speaking of
- 国際免許証 international (driver's) license
- だ am, is, are
- キーッ sound of brakes screeching
- 見せて ください please show
- ゴソゴソ sound of rummaging
- はい yes
- ここ here, this place
- に at, in, on
- あります there is, to exist
- です is, are, am
- 番号 number
- これ this one
- ですね isn't it
- 40キロ 40 kilometers per hour
- 以下 not more than
- 走る to drive
- ところ place
- いけません not good, not permitted
- すみません to be sorry

18 .... 2 すみません

OBJECTIVES:
Apologizing for mistakes, using the polite request form and more information about particles.

- 交通反則告知書 traffic violation ticket
- 青キップ blue ticket
- 書きながら while writing
- これで with/by this
- まちがい mistake
- ありません there isn't
- では then, well
- サインして ください please sign
- 反則金 fine
- 郵便局 post office
- か or
- 銀行 bank
- で at, in, on
- 払って ください please pay
- わかりました understood
- どうも very, much
- すみませんでした to be sorry (for what I did)
- これから from now on
- 気を つけて ください please be careful
- よ you know
- ○ブロローッ sound of car pulling away

CULTURE

International Driver's License

Visitors to Japan should check that they have a valid international driver's license before hitting the road in a car or on a motorcycle. Read the restrictions regarding vehicle category carefully or you may face a heavy fine. It is illegal, for example, to ride a motorcycle with a Type B passenger car license: Your license also needs to show Type A approval for two-wheel motor vehicles. To obtain an international license after arriving in Japan, submit your passport, photograph, current Japanese license, and the appropriate fee at the local licensing office. Long-term residents should remember that driving with an international license is permitted for only one year. However, national driver's licenses from most countries, including the United States and the United Kingdom, can be automatically converted to a Japanese license, subject to the requirements of the local vehicle licensing office.

PRONUNCIATION

Listen to the tape and repeat. High pitches are marked with ⌐ and low pitches with ⌐. All words appearing in **bold** should be stressed. Note that hyphenated phrases are treated as one word.

1 Sumisu-san-ga **supiido-ihan**-de keesatsu-ni tsukamatta.

Sumisu-san-no unten-menkyo-shoo-wa **kokusai-menkyo-shoo**-da.

2 **Unten-menkyo-shoo**-o misete kudasai.

3 Hai, **koko**-ni arimasu. **Kokusai-menkyo-shoo**-desu.

4 Bangoo-wa **kore**-desu-ne. Koko-wa **yon-ji-kkiro**-ika-de hashiru tokoro-desu.

Roku-ji-kkiro-wa ikemasen.

Hai, sumimasen.

6 **Kore**-de machigai arimasen-ne.

7 Dewa, koko-ni **sain**-shite kudasai. Hansoku-kin-wa **yuubinkyoku**-ka **ginkoo**-de haratte kudasai.

8 Wakarimashita. Doomo **sumimasen**-deshita.

Kore-kara-wa **ki**-o tsukete kudasai-yo.

NOTES

1 スミスさんが スピード違反で 警察に つかまった。スミスさんの 運転免許証は 国際免許証だ。
Ms. Smith was picked up by the police for speeding. Ms. Smith has an international driver's license.

❶ が here indicates the subject of a verb.

❷ で is a particle used in many ways. Here it shows that the information preceding it, スピード違反 is the reason for the action of the verb.

❸ つかまった is the plain past form of the verb つかまる.

❹ の marks a noun that modifies or possesses the following noun.

❺ は indicates the topic of the sentence. (See Notes to Module 1.)

❻ だ is the plain form of the copula and corresponds to "is" or "are."

2 運転免許証を 見せて ください。
Please show me your driver's license.

❶ を is a particle indicating the direct object, i.e. the object that receives the action of the verb.

❷ 見せて ください This is the polite request form of the verb みせる. This form comprises the て-form of the verb plus ください. In the negative, it is formed by adding -ないで to the verb stem followed by ください.

見せて ください → 見せないで ください	Please show [it] – Please don't show [it].
サインして ください → サインしないで ください	Please sign [it] – Please don't sign [it].
はらって ください → はらわないで ください	Please pay – Please don't pay.

3 はい、ここに あります。国際免許証です。
Here, it's an international driver's license.

❶ に is a particle marking the location of something or someone.

❷ あります is the polite form of the verb ある.

❸ To describe the whereabouts of an inanimate object using the particle が to mark the subject, the following structure applies:

| place | に | thing = subject | が ある / あります |

If you use the particle は to introduce the topic, the structure is as follows:

| thing (subject) = topic | は | place | に ある / あります |

However, when the subject is animate, the verb いる / います must be used instead.

| person, animal (subject) = topic | は | place | に いる / います |

Or using が to mark the subject:

| place | に | person, animal = subject | が いる / います |

To construct one sentence describing the location of several things found in different places you can use the て-form of ある (あって) or the more formal bound form (あり) to connect the two clauses.

The bound form is made by dropping the polite -ます ending of verbs.

二つめの 角の 右側に タバコ屋が あり、その 向かいに 本屋が あります。
There is a tobacco shop on the right of the second corner, and (there is) a bookstore on the opposite side of the shop. (See Task 2.)

❹ です is the polite form of the copula.

---

4 番号は これですね。ここは 40キロ以下で 走る ところです。60キロは いけません。
　——はい。すみません。
This is the number, isn't it? This is an area where you should drive within 40 kph. 60kph is not permitted.
– I understand. I am sorry.

❶ ね is a particle used when the speaker wants the listener to confirm that he or she has understood what the speaker has just said. It usually comes at the end of a sentence.

❷ 走る is in the plain form since it is used in a subordinate clause. (See Notes for Task 2 in Module 1.)

---

5 (交通反則告知書［青キップ］に 書きながら)
(While writing out a traffic violation report)

❶ 青キップ is a common name for a traffic violation ticket.

❷ 〜ながら, when added to the bound form of a verb, means "while doing 〜."
　食べながら　while eating　　飲みながら　while drinking　　歩きながら　while walking

---

6 これで まちがいありませんね。
There's no mistake here, right?

❶ これ (this) plus the particle で here means "with this" or "by this."

❷ ありません is the polite negative form of ある.

---

7 では、ここに サインして ください。反則金は 郵便局か 銀行で 払って ください。
Then sign here, please. Pay the fine at a post office or bank.

❶ A か B (か C) means A or B (or C).

❷ で is a particle that here shows where the action of the verb takes place. To indicate location of something using an intransitive verb like ある or いる, you should use the particle に.

---

8 わかりました。どうも すみませんでした。——これからは 気を つけて くださいよ。
I understand. I am very sorry. – Please be careful from now on.

❶ わかりました is the polite past form of わかる.

❷ すみませんでした is the past form of すみません.

❸ 気を つけて ください is the polite request form of the verb 気を つける.

❹ よ is a particle used here for emphasis.

DRILLS

1. 質問に 答えなさい。
   Answer the following questions.

1. だれが 警察に つかまりましたか。 → （　　　　）です。
2. スミスさんの 運転免許証は どんな 免許証ですか。 → （　　　　）です。
3. 反則金は どこで 払いますか。 → （　　　　）で 払います。

2. 次の 表を 完成させなさい。
   Complete the following chart adding the appropriate form of the verb.

	＋ください			＋ください	
かく (to write) きく (to listen)	かいて (**2**　)	(**1**　) きかないで	およぐ (to swim) いそぐ (to hurry)	およいで (**14**　)	(**13**　) いそがないで
はなす (to talk) かす (to lend)	(**3**　) かして	はなさないで (**4**　)	まつ (to wait) たつ (to stand)	(**15**　) たって	またないで (**16**　)
むすぶ (to tie) あそぶ (to play)	むすんで (**6**　)	(**5**　) あそばないで	よむ (to read) のむ (to drink)	よんで (**18**　)	(**17**　) のまないで
うる (to sell) のる (to ride)	(**7**　) のって	うらないで (**8**　)	かう (to buy) うたう (to sing)	(**19**　) うたって	かわないで (**20**　)
たべる (to eat) あける (to open)	たべて (**10**　)	(**9**　) あけないで	みる (to see) かりる (to borrow)	みて (**22**　)	(**21**　) かりないで
する (to do)	して	(**11**　)	くる (to come)	(**23**　)	こないで
いく (to go)	(**12**　)	いかないで			

VOCABULARY

- だれ　who
- つかまりました　was caught
- か　question particle
- どんな　what kind of
- どこ　where
- 払(はら)います　to pay

2 すみません……23

TASKS

1. サインの意味
The meaning of signs

次の サインの 意味は どれでしょう。正しい ものを 選んで ください。

There are fives signs on this page labeled **A** to **E**. Below is a list of three alternative explanations for each sign, but only one is correct. Look at the signs and read the sentences to select the most appropriate description of what each sign means.

A 1 ここで たばこを すって ください。
   2 ここで たばこを すわないで ください。
   3 ここで たばこを 買って ください。

B 1 この 道を 通らないで ください。
   2 こちらへ 行って ください。
   3 こちらに 有料道路が あります。

C 1 まっすぐ 行って ください。
   2 入らないで ください。
   3 車を 止めないで ください。

D 1 席が ありません。中で 休んで ください。
   2 準備を して います。少し 待って ください。
   3 休みです。また 来て ください。

E 1 トイレは こちらへ 行って ください。
   2 化粧品は ここで 買って ください。
   3 美容院は こちらに あります。

A 禁煙

B 一方通行路 →

C 立入禁止

D 休業中

E ◀ 化粧室

VOCABULARY

- 次 (つぎ)　next, following
- サイン　sign
- 意味 (いみ)　meaning
- どれ　which
- でしょう　will probably be
- 正 (ただ)しい　correct
- もの　thing, one
- 選 (えら)んで ください　please choose
- たばこ　cigarette, tobacco
- すって ください　please smoke
- すわないで ください　please don't smoke
- 買 (か)って ください　please buy
- この　this
- 道 (みち)　street, road
- 通 (とお)らないで ください　please don't pass
- こちら　this direction
- へ　to
- 行 (い)って ください　please go
- 有料道路 (ゆうりょうどうろ)　toll road
- まっすぐ　straight
- 入 (はい)らないで ください　please don't enter
- 車 (くるま)　car
- 止 (と)めないで ください　no waiting
- 席 (せき)　seat
- 中 (なか)　inside
- 休 (やす)んで ください　please rest
- 準備 (じゅんび)　preparation
- して います　is doing
- 少 (すこ)し　a little, a while
- 待 (ま)って ください　please wait
- 休 (やす)み　closed, break
- また　again
- 来 (き)て ください　please come
- トイレ　toilet, bathroom
- 化粧品 (けしょうひん)　cosmetics
- 美容院 (びよういん)　beauty parlor

2. 山田さんの 家は どれ？
Which is Mr. Yamada's house?

The following passage describes the buildings shown on the map below. Read the passage and trace the route before answering the questions.

　まず、駅から 南へ まっすぐ 行きます。二つ目の 角の 右側に たばこ屋が あり、その 向いに 本屋が あります。そこを 東に 曲がって、まっすぐ 行きます。昭和大通りを こえて、もう 少し 行くと、橋が あります。橋の 手前の 北側に レストランが あります。山田さんの 家は 橋を 渡って、南側の 二軒目です。向いは おふろ屋さんです。

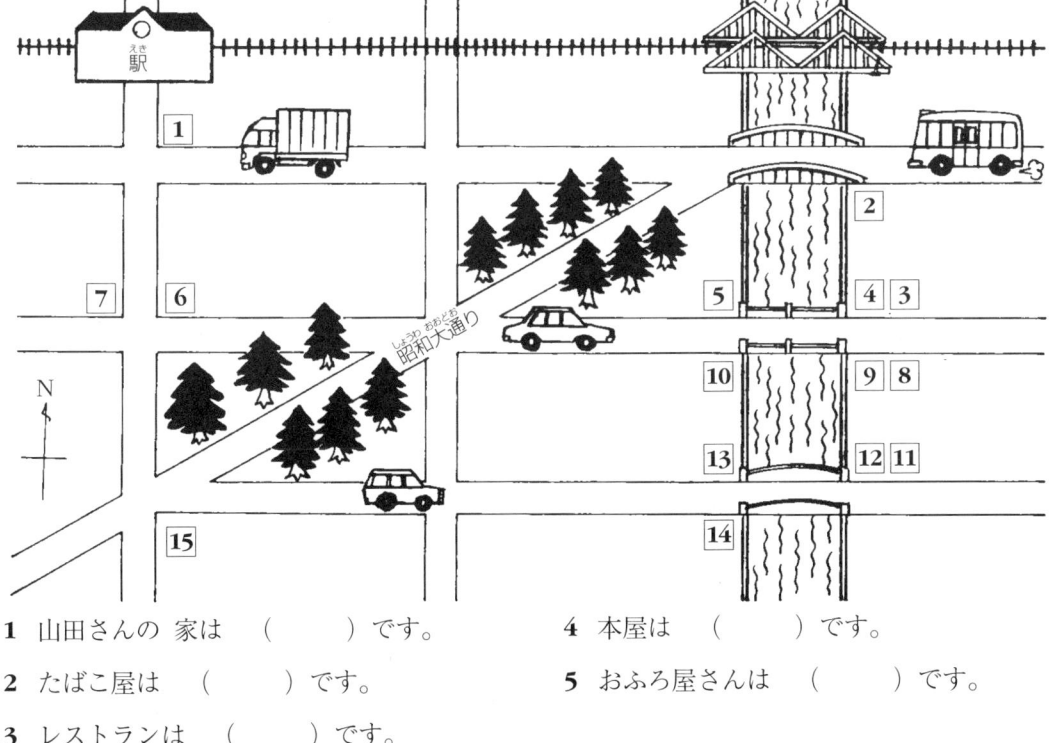

1　山田さんの 家は （　　　）です。

2　たばこ屋は （　　　）です。

3　レストランは （　　　）です。

4　本屋は （　　　）です。

5　おふろ屋さんは （　　　）です。

VOCABULARY

- まず　first, to begin with
- 駅(えき)　station
- から　from
- 南(みなみ)　south
- まっすぐ　straight
- 行(い)きます　to go
- 二(ふた)つ目(め)　second
- 角(かど)　corner
- 右側(みぎがわ)　right-hand side
- に　in, at, on
- たばこ屋(や)　tobacco shop
- あり　there being, existing
- その　that
- 向(むか)い　opposite, across
- 本屋(ほんや)　bookstore
- あります　there is, to exist
- そこ　there, that place
- を　here, particle to indicate a location along which someone/something moves
- 東(ひがし)　east
- 曲(ま)がって　turning
- 昭和大通(しょうわおおどお)り　Showa Avenue
- こえて　crossing, going over
- もう 少(すこ)し　a little more
- 橋(はし)　bridge
- 手前(てまえ)　before
- 北側(きたがわ)　north side
- レストラン　restaurant
- 渡(わた)って　crossing
- 二軒目(にけんめ)　second house: 軒 is a counter for buildings
- おふろ屋(や)さん　public bathhouse

NOTES

行(い)くと　if [you] go: Here, と attached to a sentence marks a condition that brings about what is described in the following sentence.

3 どうぞ おだいじに

Please take care of yourself.

DIALOGUE

1. スミスさんは かぜを ひいて 病院へ 行った。

2. スミスさん、どう しましたか。
3. のどが いたくて、せきが 出ます。
4. かぜを ひきましたね。 ねつは 38度5分です。

5. 頭は どうですか。いたいですか。 はい。ゆうべは 眠れませんでした。
6. では、ちゅうしゃを うちましょう。

VOCABULARY

- ○ボーッ sound-effect word for dizziness
- ●スミスさん Ms. Smith
- ●は as for, speaking of
- ●かぜを ひいて catching a cold
- ●病院 hospital
- ●へ to
- ●行った went
- ●どう how
- ●しました did
- ●のど throat
- ●いたくて being painful
- ●せきが 出ます to have a cough
- ●かぜを ひきました caught a cold
- ●ね isn't it?
- ●ねつ temperature
- ●38度5分 38.5 degrees
- ●です is, are, am
- ●頭 head
- ●いたい painful
- ●はい yes
- ●ゆうべ last night
- ●眠れませんでした couldn't sleep
- ●では then, well
- ●ちゅうしゃを うちましょう [I] will give [you] an injection
- ○ホッ sound-effect word to show relief that injection is over

OBJECTIVES:
Explaining yourself to a doctor, using adjectives and understanding the て-form.

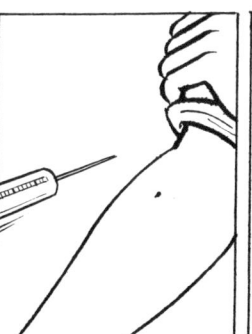

7. それから、お薬も出しましょう。うがい薬でうがいもしてください。

8. あたたかくして、お水をたくさん飲んでください。どうぞおだいじに。どうもありがとうございました。

- それから [and] then, now
- お薬 medicine
- も also
- 出しましょう [I] will give, will let out
- うがい薬 mouthwash
- で with, by means of
- うがい gargling
- して ください please do
- あたたかく して keeping ~ warm
- お水 water
- たくさん much, many
- 飲んで ください please drink
- どうぞ please
- おだいじに take care of yourself
- どうも ありがとう ございました Thank you very much (for what you did)
- ○ホーッ sound-effect word for relief

CULTURE

Hospitals and Health

A visit to a Japanese clinic can be a culturally-interesting, if time-consuming experience. Most hospitals operate a first-come-first-served-system and will not accept appointments for the first consultation. Before seeing the doctor, a nurse will usually take the patient's temperature and blood pressure, as well as ask questions about the patient's medical history. The consultation itself often takes place not in a private room, but a partitioned cubicle with thin walls or even curtains. With Japanese national health insurance, treatment is reasonably priced, although many foreign-owned practices will only accept private insurance. Hospitalization in Japan customarily requires family members to attend to the patient's personal care such as bathing and meal-serving duties. Moreover, when entering or leaving hospital it is usual to give gifts to the nurses and physician-in-charge.

PRONUNCIATION

Listen to the tape and repeat. High pitches are marked with ⌈ and low pitches with ⌉. All words appearing in **bold** should be stressed. Note that hyphenated phrases are treated as one word.

1. Sumisu-san-wa kaze-o hiite, **byooin**-e itta.

2. Sumisu-san, **doo**-shimashita-ka.

3. Nodo-ga itakute, **seki**-ga demasu.

4. **Kaze**-o hikimashita-ne.

   Netsu-wa **san-juu-hachi-do-go-bu**-desu.

5. **Atama**-wa doo-desu-ka. **Itai**-desu-ka.

   Hai, yuube-wa **nemuremasen**-deshita.

6. Dewa, **chuusha**-o uchimashoo.

7. Sorekara, **o-kusuri**-mo dashimashoo. Ugai-gusuri-de ugai-mo shite kudasai.

8. Atatakaku shite, o-mizu-o **takusan** nonde kudasai. Doozo **o-daiji**-ni.

   Doomo **arigatoo**-gozaimashita.

NOTES

1 スミスさんは かぜを ひいて、病院へ 行った。
Ms. Smith went to the hospital because she caught a cold.

❶ は indicates the topic of the sentence. (See Notes to Module 1.)

❷ かぜを ひいて This is the て-form of かぜを ひく, used here to connect the two clauses. The て-form of verbs can be either て or で depending on the verb type. (See Notes and Drills in Module 2.)

The て-form of adjectives is made by dropping the い of い-adjectives and adding -くて, or adding で to な-adjectives or the copula だ.
Verbs：食べる(to eat) – 食べて　　飲む(to drink) – 飲んで
Adjectives：新しい(new) – 新しくて　　元気な(fine, well) – 元気で
With copula だ(is, are)：先生だ(to be a teacher) – 先生で

The て-form of verbs and adjectives is used to connect a sentence as follows:
あたたかく して、お水を たくさん 飲んで ください。(See 8.)
のどが いたくて、せきが 出ます。(See 3.)
父は 元気で、まだ 働いて います。
My father is fine and is still working.
田中さんは 先生で、中学校で 数学を 教えて います。
Mr./Ms. Tanaka is a teacher and is teaching mathematics at a junior high school.

❸ へ is a particle that here shows physical direction.

❹ 行った is the plain past form of the verb 行く.

2 スミスさん、どう しましたか。
What is the problem, Ms. Smith?

❶ しました is the polite past form of する.

❷ か is a particle that functions like a question mark here.

3 のどが いたくて、せきが 出ます。
My throat hurts and I have a cough.

❶ が is a particle that here introduces the subject.

❷ いたくて is the て-form of the い-adjective いたい.

❸ せきが 出ます is the polite form of the verb せきが 出る.

4 かぜを ひきましたね。——ねつは 38度 5分です。
I see that you have caught a cold. –You have a temperature of 38.5 degrees.

❶ かぜを ひきました is the polite past form of the verb かぜを ひく.

❷ ね is a particle used when the speaker is confirming something.

5 頭は どうですか。いたいですか。——はい。ゆうべは 眠れませんでした。
How is your head? Does it hurt? –Yes. I couldn't sleep last night.

❶ いたい is an い-adjective.

❷ 眠れませんでした is the polite past negative form of the verb 眠る in its potential form 眠れる.

6 では、ちゅうしゃを うちましょう。
[I] will give [you] an injection.

ちゅうしゃを うちましょう This is the polite -ましょう form of うつ. This form shows intention of the speaker to do something.

7 それから、お薬も 出しましょう。うがい薬で うがいも して ください。
And now I'll also prescribe you some medicine. Please gargle with this mouthwash too.

❶ お薬 is a polite way of saying 薬.

❷ も is a particle that comes after the noun, here, to mean "also."
出しましょう is the -ましょう form of 出す.

❸ で is a particle that means "with" or "by" when it follows a noun.

❹ うがいも して ください is the polite request form of うがいを する. (See Notes and Drills in Module 2.) Note that the particle も displaces the を.

8 あたたかく して、お水を たくさん 飲んで ください。どうぞ おだいじに。
——どうも ありがとう ございました。
Keep warm and drink lots of water. Take care of yourself. –Thank you very much.

❶ あたたかく して is the て-form of あたたかく する.

❷ お水 is the polite way of saying 水.

❸ 飲んで ください is the polite request form of 飲む.

❹ どうぞ おだいじに is used to wish a sick person a speedy recovery.

DRILLS

1. 質問に 答えなさい。
Answer the following questions.

1. だれが かぜを ひきましたか。 → （　　　　　）です。
2. スミス さんは どこへ 行きましたか。 → （　　　　　）へ 行きました。
3. スミス さんの ねつは 何度 何分でしたか。 → （　　　　　）でした。
4. お医者さんは 何を しましたか。 → （　　　　　）を うちました。
   それから （　　　　　）も 出しました。

2. 例に ならって、文を くみあわせなさい。
Combine the sentences as shown in the examples.

●頭が いたい　　●ねつが ある　　●のどが いたい

●体が だるい　　●せきが 出る　　●さむけが する

●食欲が ない　　●おなかが いたい　　●はなが 出る

VOCABULARY

- ●だれ who
- ●どこ where
- ●行(い)きました went
- ●の of
- ●何度(なんど) 何分(なんぷ) what degrees [in temperature]
- ●でした was, were
- ●お医者(いしゃ)さん doctor
- ●何(なに、なん) what
- ●しました did
- ●うちました gave [an injection]
- ●出(だ)しました prescribed [medicine]
- ●ある to have, there is
- ●体(からだ) body
- ●だるい to feel tired, weak
- ●せきが 出(で)る to have a cough
- ●さむけが する to have a chill
- ●食欲(しょくよく)が ない to have no appetite
- ●おなかが いたい to have a stomach ache
- ●はなが 出(で)る to have a runny nose
- ●例(れい) example
- ●(いたいです)が (it is painful,) but
- ●ありません not to have
- ●いたく ありません not painful

1

【例】 頭が いたくて、ねつが あります。
　　　 ねつが あって、のどが いたいです。
　　　 のどが いたくて、体が だるいです。

1 体が ＿＿＿。

2 せきが ＿＿＿。

3 さむけが ＿＿＿＿＿＿＿＿＿＿＿＿＿＿＿＿＿＿＿＿＿＿＿＿＿＿＿＿＿＿＿＿＿＿＿＿＿＿＿。

4 食欲が ＿＿。

5 おなかが ＿＿＿＿＿＿＿＿＿＿＿＿＿＿＿＿＿＿＿＿＿＿＿＿＿＿＿＿＿＿＿＿＿＿＿＿＿＿＿。

6 はなが ＿＿。

2

【例】 頭が いたくて、ねつが あって、のどが いたいです。
　　　 ねつが あって、のどが いたくて、体が だるいです。
　　　 のどが いたくて、体が だるくて、せきが 出ます。

1 体が ＿＿＿。

2 せきが ＿＿＿。

3 さむけが ＿＿＿＿＿＿＿＿＿＿＿＿＿＿＿＿＿＿＿＿＿＿＿＿＿＿＿＿＿＿＿＿＿＿＿＿＿＿＿。

4 食欲が ＿＿。

5 おなかが ＿＿＿＿＿＿＿＿＿＿＿＿＿＿＿＿＿＿＿＿＿＿＿＿＿＿＿＿＿＿＿＿＿＿＿＿＿＿＿。

6 はなが ＿＿。

3

【例】 頭は いたいですが、ねつは ありません。
　　　 ねつは ありますが、のどは いたく ありません。
　　　 のどは いたいですが、体は だるく ありません。

1 体は ＿＿＿。

2 せきは ＿＿＿。

3 さむけは ＿＿＿＿＿＿＿＿＿＿＿＿＿＿＿＿＿＿＿＿＿＿＿＿＿＿＿＿＿＿＿＿＿＿＿＿＿＿＿。

4 食欲は ＿＿。

5 おなかは ＿＿＿＿＿＿＿＿＿＿＿＿＿＿＿＿＿＿＿＿＿＿＿＿＿＿＿＿＿＿＿＿＿＿＿＿＿＿＿。

6 はなは ＿＿。

TASK

誰が いちばん よく 歩いたか。
Who has walked the furthest?

たくさん 歩いた 順に 名前を 並べなさい。
Write in the walkers' names in the appropriate order.

上田さん、山下さん、中島さん、岡島さんは それぞれ 午前中に 家を 出て、午後 帰りました。
午前中は A、B、Cの 所は 工事中で、通れません。午後は 通れます。

1 上田さんは ケーキ屋さんと 肉屋さんへ 行き、午後 帰りました。
2 山下さんは 学校で 先生に 会って、午後から スポーツ用品店と お寺へ 行って、帰りました。
3 中島さんは 銀行で お金を おろして、レストランで 食事を して、午後 デパートに 寄って、帰りました。
4 岡島さんは 神社へ お参りしてから、午後 病院へ 行きました。

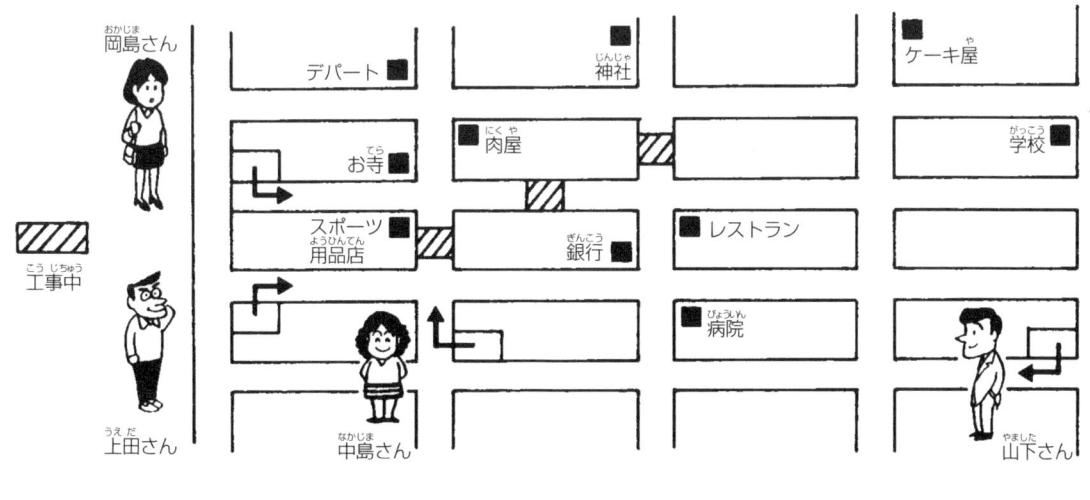

1   2   3   4

VOCABULARY

- たくさん much
- 歩(ある)いた walked
- 順(じゅん)に in order
- 名前(なまえ) name
- 並(なら)べなさい arrange: an imperative form
- 上田(うえだ)、山下(やました)、中島(なかじま)、岡島(おかじま) are all family names
- それぞれ each
- 午前中(ごぜんちゅう) in the morning
- に at, in
- 家(いえ、うち) house, home
- を here, particle to indicate a departing place
- 出(で)て leaving
- 午後(ごご) [in the] afternoon
- 帰(かえ)りました returned [home]
- 所(ところ) place
- 工事中(こうじちゅう) under construction
- で being
- 通(とお)れません cannot pass
- 通(とお)れます can pass
- ケーキ屋(や) cake shop, bakery
- 肉屋(にくや) butcher
- 行(い)き going
- 学校(がっこう) school
- 先生(せんせい) teacher
- 〜に 会(あ)って meeting 〜
- スポーツ用品店(ようひんてん) sports shop
- お寺(てら) temple
- 行(い)って going
- 銀行(ぎんこう) bank
- お金(かね) money
- おろして withdrawing
- レストラン restaurant
- 食事(しょくじ)を して having a meal
- デパート department store
- 〜に 寄(よ)って dropping in 〜
- 神社(じんじゃ) shrine
- お参(まい)りして visiting [a shrine/temple]
- 〜て から after [doing] 〜
- 病院(びょういん) hospital
- 行(い)きました went

4 ありがとう ございました　　Thank you.

DIALOGUE

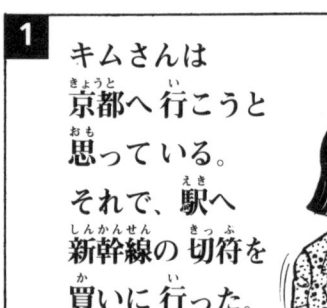
1. キムさんは京都へ行こうと思っている。それで、駅へ新幹線の切符を買いに行った。

2. 7月24日午前10時4分東京発のひかり11号で京都へ行きたいのですが。

3. ええっと、7月24日午前10時4分ひかり11号京都まで1枚ですね。指定席ですか、自由席ですか。

4. 指定席をください。ああ、それから禁煙席をおねがいします。

5. はい。7月24日ひかり11号10時4分京都まで。禁煙席は7号車の5D。

6. 乗車料金が7830円と特急料金が5140円で、合計1万2970円です。片道ですね。

VOCABULARY

- ●キムさん Ms. Kim
- ●は as for, speaking of
- ●京都へ to Kyoto
- ●行こう to intend to go
- ●と that
- ●思って いる is thinking
- ●それで so, then
- ●駅 station
- ●新幹線 the Shinkansen super express train
- ●の of
- ●切符 ticket
- ●買いに in order to buy
- ●行った went
- ●7月24日 July 24th
- ●午前10時4分 10:04 A.M.
- ●東京発 departing from Tokyo
- ●ひかり11号 the Hikari No. 11
- ●で by
- ●行きたい to want to go
- ●が but
- ●ええっと well, er, let me see
- ●まで as far as, up to, till
- ●枚 counter for thin, flat units
- ●です is, are, am
- ●ね isn't it?
- ●指定席 reserved seat
- ●自由席 unreserved seat

OBJECTIVES:
Saying thank you, expressing one's intentions and telling others what one wants to do.

- ●ください please give
- ●ああ Oh! Ah!
- ●それから [and] then, well
- ●禁煙席 nonsmoking seat
- ●おねがいします please [give me]
- ●はい yes, certainly
- ●7号車 car no. 7
- ○ピッピッ computer noise
- ●乗車料金 fare
- ●円 yen
- ●と and
- ●特急料金 charge for the super express
- ●で being
- ●合計 [in] total
- ●1万 ten thousand
- ●片道 one-way [ticket]
- ●往復 round-trip [ticket]
- ●帰り returning
- ●行き going
- ●ぜんぶで in all, altogether
- ○ゴソゴソ sound-effect word for rummaging
- ●これで with/by this
- ●出す to put out, to give
- ●おつり change
- ●ありがとう ございました
   Thank you [for what you did]

4 ありがとう ございました

CULTURE

Traveling by Train

Subways and railroads are generally fast, frequent, clean, and convenient. Tickets must be purchased before starting your journey from one of the many vending machines located near the station entrance. Although some machines can provide change for ¥10,000 and ¥5,000 bills, most accept ¥1,000 bills, and coins of all denominations except ¥5 and ¥1. A nearby money-changing machine or station employee will break up larger bills at your convenience. As well as standard one-way tickets, commuters can buy season tickets or regular tickets in bulk, and the larger stations sell tickets for people who merely want to see a friend or relative off from the platform. Special features on Japanese trains include the "Green Car" first class reserved car on express trains like the *Shinkansen*, and the "Silver Seat" in the commuter trains for the aged or physically challenged.

PRONUNCIATION

Listen to the tape and repeat. High pitches are marked with ⌐ and low pitches with ¬. All words appearing in **bold** should be stressed. Note that hyphenated phrases are treated as one word.

1. Kimu-san-wa **Kyooto**-e ikoo-to omotte iru. Sorede, eki-e Shinkansen-no kippu-o kai-ni itta.

2. Shichi-gatsu ni-juu-yokka gozen juu-ji yon-pun Tookyoo-hatsu-no Hikari-juu-ichi-goo-de **Kyooto**-e ikitai-no-desu-ga.

3. Eetto...shichi-gatsu ni-juu-yokka...gozen juu-ji yon-pun...Hikari-juu-ichi-goo...**Kyooto**-made... **ichi-mai**-desu-ne. **Shitee-seki**-desu-ka, **jiyuu-seki**-desu-ka.

4. **Shitee-seki**-o kudasai. Aa, sorekara **kin'en-seki**-o onegaishimasu.

5. Hai. Shichi-gatsu ni-juu-yokka...Hikari-juu-ichi-goo...Juu-ji yon-pun...Kyooto-made...Kin'en-seki-wa nana-goo-sha-no goo-dii.

6. Joosharyookin-ga nana-sen-happyaku-san-juu-en-to tokkyuu-ryookin-ga go-sen-hyaku-yon-juu-en-de, gookee **ichi-man-ni-sen-kyuu-hyaku-nana-juu-en**-desu. Katamichi-desu-ne.

7. A, **oofuku**-desu. Kaeri-wa **jiyuu-seki**-o kudasai.

8. Hai, oofuku ... iki-wa shitei-seki-de, kaeri-wa jiyuu-seki...Zenbu-de **ni-man-go-sen-yon-hyaku-yon-juu-en**-desu-ne.

9. **Kore**-de onegaishimasu. **Yon-sen-go-hyaku-roku-juu-en**-no otsuri-desu. **Arigatoo** gozaimashita.

NOTES

1 キムさんは 京都へ 行こうと 思って いる。それで、駅へ 新幹線の 切符を 買いに 行った。
Ms. Kim plans to go to Kyoto. So she went to the station to buy a ticket for the Shinkansen super express train.

❶ は is a particle introducing the topic of the sentence. (See Notes to Module 1.)

❷ へ is a particle that here shows physical direction.

❸ 行こう is the [y]oo form of 行く indicating intention.

❹ と is a quotation particle, often followed by the verb 思う (to think.)
   キムさんは 京都へ 行こうと 思って いる。(行く→行こう)
   私は 今晩 タイ料理を 食べようと 思って います。(食べる→食べよう)
   I think I will eat Thai food tonight.

❺ 思って いる is the -て いる form of 思う.

❻ Here the particle の qualifies the following noun [切符] with the preceding noun [新幹線].

❼ In this sentence, the particle を indicates the direct object [切符] of the verb.

❽ 買いに　Here the particle に expresses purpose—"in order to buy."

❾ 行った is the plain past form of 行く.

2 7月 24日 午前 10時 4分 東京発の ひかり 11号で 京都へ 行きたいのですが。
I want to go to Kyoto by Hikari No. 11 departing from Tokyo at 10:04 a.m. on July 24th.

❶ Here, で indicates the mode of travel.
   車で 行こう　Let's go by car.

❷ 行きたい is the so-called -たい form of the verb 行く used here to mean "[I] want to go." Attached to a verb stem, the bound form, the -たい form normally expresses the speaker's own wish or desire to do something.
   私は ビールが 飲みたいです。(飲む→飲みたい)　I'd like to drink beer.

❸ Added to the end of a sentence, -のです／-のだ and the more informal -んです／-んだ make what is being said more colloquial, as well as emphatic and explanatory. In this case, it also softens the preceding statement of desire and therefore makes the speaker's wish polite.
   どこへ 行きたいのですか。　Where would you like to go?
   アフリカへ 行きたいんです。　I'd like to go to Africa.

❹ が, here, is a conjunction meaning weak "but." It is common to use が to imply something that is not actually said.

3 ええっと、7月 24日 午前 10時 4分 ひかり 11号 京都まで 1枚ですね。
指定席ですか、自由席ですか。
Let me see...July 24th...10:04 A.M...Hikari No. 11...to Kyoto...one ticket, right? Would you like to reserve a seat?

❶ 枚 is the counter for thin, flat objects like tickets, paper, shirts, etc.

❷ です is the polite form of the copula.

- ❸ ね is a particle used by the speaker for confirmation.
- ❹ か acts as a question mark at the end of a sentence.

---

4 指定席を ください。ああ、それから 禁煙席を おねがいします。
I'd like to reserve a seat, please. Oh, and could I have a seat in a nonsmoking car, please?

- ❶ ください means "please give [me]."
- ❷ おねがいします is a polite way of asking for something or asking someone to do something.

---

5 はい。7月 24日 ひかり 11号 10時 4分 京都まで。禁煙席は 7号車の 5D。
Certainly. July 24th...Hikari No. 11...10:04 A.M....to Kyoto...seat 5D in non-smoking car no.7.

---

6 乗車料金が 7830円と 特急料金が 5140円で、合計 1万 2970円です。片道ですね。
The standard fare of ¥7,830 plus a surplus charge for the super express of ¥5,140 comes to a total fare of ¥12,970. Will that be one-way only?

- ❶ が marks the subjects [乗車料金 and 特急料金] of this sentence.
- ❷ The two nouns are joined by the particle と, meaning "and."
- ❸ Here で is not a particle, but the て-form of the copula, used here to connect the two clauses.

---

7 あ、往復です。帰りは 自由席を ください。
Oh, a round-trip ticket please. I don't want to reserve a seat for the return trip.

- ❶ あ is an exclamation similar to "oh" or "um."
- ❷ 往復 and 自由席 are common abbreviations of the longer phrases, 往復の 切符 and 自由席の 切符. The omission of 切符 causes no confusion among Japanese as it is obvious from the context that the speaker is referring to tickets.

---

8 はい、往復。行きは 指定席で、帰りは 自由席。ぜんぶで 2万 5440円ですね。
Certainly. Round trip...reserving a seat on the outbound but not on the return journey. The total is ¥25,440.

ぜんぶで means "altogether."

---

9 これで おねがいします。(3万円を 出す。)
──4560円の おつりです。ありがとう ございました。
Here you are (gives ¥30,000.) –Your change is ¥4,560. Thank you very much.

- ❶ これで means "with this" or "by this."
- ❷ ありがとう ございました is used when thanking someone for something that they have already done for you.

DRILLS

1. 質問に 答えなさい。
Answer the following questions.

1　キムさんは どこへ 行こうと 思って いますか。
　→　（　　　　　　）へ 行こうと 思っています。

2　ひかり 11号は 東京発 何時 何分の 新幹線ですか。
　→　午前（　　）時（　　）分 の新幹線です。

3　特急 料金は いくらでしたか。　→　（　　　　　　）でした。

4　帰りは 指定席ですか、自由席ですか。　→　（　　　　　　）です。

2. 次の 会話を 完成させなさい。
Supply the missing words to complete the following dialogues.

1　(a) どうして （1. was absent）んですか。
　 (b) 頭が （2. was painful）んです。

2　(a) 田中さんは もう 結婚して いますよ。
　 (b) そうですか、（3. is married）んですか。

3　(a) きのう ディズニーランドへ （4. went）んだ。
　 (b) へえ、どうだった。

4　(a) すみません、この 本を （5. want to borrow）のですが…。
　 (b) いいですよ、どうぞ。

5　(a) よく がんばりますね。
　 (b) ええ、お金を ためて、旅行を しようと （6. is thinking）んです。

VOCABULARY

- どこ where
- 思(おも)って います is thinking
- 何時(なんじ) 何分(なんぷん) what time: 何時[what o'clock] + 何分[what minutes]
- いくら how much
- でした was, were
- どうして why
- 休(やす)んだ was absent
- 頭(あたま) head
- いたかった was painful
- 田中(たなか)さん Mr./Ms. Tanaka
- もう already
- 結婚(けっこん)して います is married
- よ you know
- そうですか is that right?
- きのう yesterday
- ディズニーランド Disneyland
- へえ dear me! really?
- どう how
- だった was
- すみません excuse me
- この this
- 本(ほん) book
- 借(か)りたい to want to borrow
- いい OK, good
- どうぞ please
- よく well, hard
- がんばります try hard
- ええ yes
- お金(かね) money
- ためて saving
- 旅行(りょこう) trip, travel
- しよう to intend to do

T A S K S

1. だれが 何(なに)を いくつ 買(か)ったか。
 Who bought what and how many?

バザーが 3日間(かかん) ありました。3日目(かめ)の 4時(じ)に 次(つぎ)の 物(もの)が 残(のこ)りました。佐藤(さとう)さんと キムさんと 林(りん)さんと スミスさんが その 残(のこ)り物(もの)を ぜんぶ 買(か)いました。

〈?〉の 数字(すうじ)も 考(かんが)えて、読(よ)み方(かた)を ぜんぶ 書(か)き入(い)れて ください。

There was a three-day sale recently. At 4:00 P.M. on the third and last day of the sale, the following items had been left unsold. Between themselves, Sato, Kim, Lin, and Smith bought all of the remaining items. The chart below gives clues to who bought how many of what. Supply the missing numbers and write in the correct "counters."

【残(のこ)り物(もの)】　本(ほん)…22冊(さつ)　くつした…11足(そく)　音楽(おんがく)テープ…24本(ほん)　ハンカチ…20枚(まい)

〈佐藤さん〉
くつした　　　〈2〉　(**1**　　　　)
本　　　　　　〈9〉　(**2**　　　　)
ハンカチ　　　〈?〉　(**3**　　　　)
音楽テープ　　〈10〉 (**4**　　　　)

〈キムさん〉
ハンカチ　　　〈2〉　(**5**　　　　)
音楽テープ　　〈?〉　(**6**　　　　)
くつした　　　〈5〉　(**7**　　　　)
本　　　　　　〈8〉　(**8**　　　　)

〈林さん〉
本　　　　　　〈?〉　(**9**　　　　)
くつした　　　〈3〉　(**10**　　　)
音楽テープ　　〈5〉　(**11**　　　)
ハンカチ　　　〈4〉　(**12**　　　)

〈スミスさん〉
ハンカチ　　　〈7〉　(**13**　　　)
音楽テープ　　〈6〉　(**14**　　　)
くつした　　　〈?〉　(**15**　　　)
本　　　　　　〈1〉　(**16**　　　)

VOCABULARY

- バザー　bazaar
- 3日間 (みっかかん)　(for) three days
- ありました　was held, there was
- 3日目 (みっかめ)　the third day
- 4時 (よじ) に　at 4 o'clock
- 次 (つぎ)　following, next
- 物 (もの)　thing, article
- 残 (のこ) りました　remaind
- 佐藤 (さとう) (Sato), キム(Kim), 林 (りん) (Lin), スミス(Smith) are all family names.
- その　that
- 残 (のこ) り物 (もの)　the rest, the remainder
- 全部　all
- 買 (か) いました　bought
- 数字 (すうじ)　number, figure
- も　also
- 考 (かんが) えて　thinking
- 読 (よ) み方 (かた)　how to read
- 書 (か) き入 (い) れて ください　please write in
- 冊 (さつ)　counter for bound units such as books and magazines
- くつした　socks
- 足 (そく、ぞく)　pair: counter for socks, shoes, and the like
- 音楽 (おんがく) テープ　music tape
- 本 (ほん、ぼん、ぽん)　counter for long, cylindrical units including cassette tapes
- ハンカチ　handkerchief

2. だれが 食堂車に いちばん 近いか。
Who is sitting the closest to the dining car?

のぼるさん、スーザンさん、インディラさん、カールさん、ホセさん、モハメッドさん、ジャネットさんが 新幹線の ひかり号で 東京から 京都へ 行きました。

Noboru, Susan, Indila, Carl, Jose, Mohammed, and Janet travelled on the Shinkansen super express train from Tokyo to Kyoto. Read the clues below and answer the questions at the end.

1 インディラさんと スーザンさんは 別の 禁煙車に 乗りました。
2 ジャネットさんと ホセさんは スーザンさんから 5つ うしろの 禁煙車に 乗りました。
3 モハメッドさんは インディラさんの すぐ 前の 禁煙車に 乗りました。
4 のぼるさんは インディラさんから 3つ うしろの 車両に すわりました。
5 カールさんは のぼるさんと スーザンさんの 間の 車両に 乗りました。
6 だれも グリーン車には 乗りませんでした。
7 ジャネットさんと ホセさんだけが 同じ 車両です。

注： a ひかり号には 1号車から 16号車まで あります。
　　 b 自由席は 1号車から 5号車までで、あとは 指定席です。
　　 c 自由席は 指定席より 500円 やすいです。
　　 d 指定席の 9号車と 10号車は グリーン車です。
　　 e 禁煙車は 1号車、2号車、7号車、10号車、12号車です。
　　 f 食堂車は 8号車です。

京都←	禁	禁					禁	食堂車	グリーン	禁グリーン	禁	禁					→東京
	1	2	3	4	5	6	7	8	9	10	11	12	13	14	15	16	

←―――自由席―――→　←―――指定席―――→

質問： 1 だれが 食堂車に いちばん 近いですか。
　　　 2 だれと だれが たばこを すいますか。
　　　 3 のぼるさんの 切符と ホセさんの 切符と どちらの ほうが 高いですか。

VOCABULARY

- ひかり号（ごう） the super express train Hikari
- から from
- 行（い）きました went
- 別（べつ） other, another
- 禁煙車（きんえんしゃ） nonsmoking car
- ～に 乗（の）りました got on ～
- うしろ back, behind
- すぐ just, right
- 前（まえ） front, ahead
- 車両（しゃりょう） car
- すわりました sat
- ～と～の 間（あいだ） between ～ and ～
- だれも + negative nobody
- グリーン車（しゃ） the green [first class] car
- 乗（の）りませんでした didn't get on
- だけ only, just
- 同（おな）じ same
- 注（ちゅう） notes
- ひかり号（ごう）には with the Hikari train
- あります there is, to have
- あと the rest
- より [more] than
- やすい cheap
- 食堂車（しょくどうしゃ） dining car
- 質問（しつもん） question
- だれ who
- いちばん most, to the greatest degree
- 近（ちか）い close, near
- たばこ cigarette, tobacco
- すいます to smoke
- ～と～と between ～ and ～
- どちらの ほう which one
- 高（たか）い expensive

5 かんぱい   Cheers!

DIALOGUE

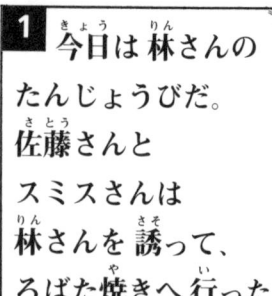

1 今日は林さんのたんじょうびだ。佐藤さんとスミスさんは林さんを誘って、ろばた焼きへ行った。

2 スミスさん：肉と魚とどちらが好き？

3 肉のほうが好きです。リブを注文するわ。佐藤さんは？

4 ぼくは魚だな。かれいがいちばんいいんだ。それから、焼きなすも。

林さんは？

VOCABULARY

- 今日 today
- は as for, speaking of
- 林さん Mr. Lin
- の of
- たんじょうび birthday
- だ is, are, am
- 佐藤さん Mr. Sato
- と and
- スミスさん Ms. Smith
- 誘って inviting
- ろばた焼き robatayaki restaurant
- へ to
- 行った went
- ○ワハハ、ハハハ sound-effect word for laughter
- 肉 meat
- 魚 fish
- どちら which one [of the two]
- 好き to like
- ほう alternative
- です is, are, am
- リブ spareribs
- 注文する to order
- わ particle used by a female speaker to express her weak assertion or volition
- ぼく [masculine] I
- な you know
- かれい flatfish
- いちばん most, to the greatest degree, no.1
- いい good

OBJECTIVES:
Expressing congratulations, using comparatives and superlatives.

- ●んだ you know
- ●それから [and] then, well
- ●焼きなす grilled eggplant
- ●も also
- ○じーっ word to show that Mr. Lin is studying the menu
- ●そうですね Let me see
- ●焼き鳥 skewered chicken
- ●いか squid, cuttlefish
- ●いただきます to have, to receive
- ●ほんとうに really, truly
- ●ありがとう Thank you
- ○サッ word to show beer glasses are being picked up and held out
- ●かんぱいに for drinking a toast
- ●お酒 sake, liquor
- ●より [more] than
- ●いい good
- ●ね isn't it?
- ●さ OK, now, come on
- ●かんぱいしよう Let's make a toast
- ●おたんじょうび おめでとう Happy Birthday!
- ●かんぱーい！ Cheers!
- ●どうも very, much
- ○パチパチ、パチパチッ sound-effect word for clapping

CULTURE

Oshibori

Whether dining at Tokyo's richest restaurant or grabbing a quick snack from a tiny back-street noodle bar, customers can expect to be offered a glass of iced water and a wet hand towel, heated in winter and chilled in summer, soon after being seated at the table or counter. As well as wiping their fingers clean in preparation for their meal, a lot of men will use the *oshibori* to refresh their face and neck, especially in the hot and humid summer. Women, however, are more likely to neatly fold up the *oshibori* after wiping their hands. At the end of the day, the restaurant or coffee shop will send their hand towels to a special laundry. Cleaned towels, sealed in polypropylene, are delivered the following morning. Many coffee shops now provide disposable, prepackaged wet tissues instead of traditional *oshibori*. Passengers flying with Japanese and some other airlines will also be given *oshibori* to refresh themselves during long flights.

PRONUNCIATION

Listen to the tape and repeat. High pitches are marked with ⌈ and low pitches with ⌉. All words appearing in **bold** should be stressed. Note that hyphenated phrases are treated as one word.

1 Kyoo-wa Rin-san-no **tanjoobi**-da. Satoo-san-to Sumisu-san-wa Rin-san-o sasotte, **robatayaki**-e itta.

2 Sumisu-san-wa niku-to sakana-to **dochira**-ga suki?

3 Niku-no hoo-ga suki-desu. **Ribu**-o chuumon-suru-wa. Satoo-san-wa?

4 Boku-wa **sakana**-da-na. **Karee**-ga ichiban ii-n-da. Sorekara, **yakinasu**-mo. Rin-san-wa?

5 Soo-desu-ne, boku-wa **yakitori**-to **ika**-o itadakimasu. Kyoo-wa hontoo-ni **arigatoo**.

6 Kampai-ni-wa o-sake-yori **biiru**-ga ii-ne. Sa, **kampai**-shiyoo.

7 O-tanjoobi **omedotoo**. Kampaai!

Doomo **arigatoo**.

NOTES

1 今日は 林さんの たんじょうびだ。佐藤さんと スミスさんは 林さんを 誘って、ろばた焼きへ 行った。
Today is Mr. Lin's birthday. Mr. Sato and Ms. Smith have invited out Mr. Lin to a robatayaki restaurant.

❶ The particle は introduces the topic of the sentence. (See Notes to Module 1.)

❷ Here the particle の marks the noun modifiying the following noun.

❸ と is a particle that here joins nouns in the same way as "and."

❹ を is a particle to indicate the direct object of the verb.

❺ 誘って is the て-form of the verb 誘う (to invite), used here to connect the clauses.

❻ へ is a particle used here to show direction.

---

2 スミスさんは 肉と 魚と どちらが 好き？
Ms. Smith, which do you prefer, meat or fish?

❶ どちら means "which."

❷ Here the particle が introduces the direct object of 好き.

❸ 好き is a な-adjective meaning "to like."

2 and **3** (see below) are examples of comparison. The typical structure is as follows: (words in parentheses are optional: their position can change or they can be left out altogether if the meaning is clear.)

(i) Aと Bと どちら(の ほう)が おもしろいですか。
 Which is more interesting, A or B?

(ii) B (の ほう)が Aより おもしろいです。
 B is more interesting than A.

(iii) スミスさんは 肉と 魚と どちらが 好き。(See above.)

(iv) 肉の ほうが 好きです。(See **3**.)

(v) かんぱいには お酒より ビールが いいね。(See **6**.)

---

3 肉の ほうが 好きです。リブを 注文するわ。佐藤さんは？
I prefer meat. So I'll order ribs. How about you, Mr. Sato?

❶ ほう is used here optionally after the noun identified as the preferred item.

❷ わ is a particle used at the end of a statement by a female speaker to express her weak assertion or volition.

4 ぼくは 魚だな。かれいが いちばん いいんだ。それから、焼きなすも。林さんは？
I'll have fish. The flatfish is the best. I'll also have grilled eggplant. How about you, Mr. Lin?

❶ ぼく is used by men as the personal pronoun, "I."

❷ な is used here by the male speaker, Mr. Sato, to confirm his preference for fish. It is used in a similar way with the same meaning as ね, but rarely by female speakers.

❸ いちばん followed by an adjective expresses the superlative, ie. the biggest, the strongest, etc. Here, it preceeds the い-adjective いい(good), making its meaning "best."

　Aと Bと Cの 中で どれが いちばん おもしろいですか。
Which is the most interesting among A, B, and C?

Note that in comparisons of more than two things, どれ is used instead of どちら.

❹ いいんだ　Adding んだ to the end of a sentence makes it more colloquial, emphatic, and explanatory. (See **2**-❸ in Notes to Module 4.)

❺ も is a particle that here means "also."

5 そうですね、ぼくは 焼き鳥と いかを いただきます。今日は ほんとうに ありがとう。
Let me see...I'll have yakitori and squid. Thank you so much for today.

いただきます is the polite -ます form of いただく(to have, to receive). It is also a common-used expression spoken immediately before eating.

6 かんぱいには お酒より ビールが いいね。さ、かんぱいしよう。
Beer is better than sake for a toast, don't you think? OK, let's have a toast.

❶ Here the particle に is used to show purpose.

❷ お酒 is a polite way of saying 酒.

❸ ね is a particle used when the speaker (male or female) is confirming something.

❹ かんぱいしよう is the [y]oo form of the verb かんぱいする. (See **1** in Notes to Module 4.)

7 おたんじょうび おめでとう。かんぱーい！── どうも ありがとう。
Happy birthday! Cheers! – Thank you.

おめでとう means "congratulations" and can be used at many celebrations such as birthdays and weddings. The more formal expression is おめでとう ございます.

In Japanese there is an abundance of set congratulatory phrases for different occasions. For example: おかえりなさい (Welcome home!) is used to toast someone who has been away for a while. おつかれさまでした is used to thank somebody for their (successful) efforts.

DRILLS

1. 質問に 答えなさい。
Answer the following questions.

1 今日は だれの たんじょうびですか。
→ （　　　　）の たんじょうびです。

2 林さんと 佐藤さんと スミスさんは どこへ 行きましたか。
→ （　　　　）へ 行きました。

3 スミスさんは 肉と 魚と どちらが 好きですか。
→ （　　　　）の ほうが 好きです。

4 佐藤さんは 何が いちばん 好きですか。
→ （　　　　）が いちばん 好きです。

2. 正しい ほうを 選びなさい。
Complete the seven sentences below by selecting the most appropriate adjective.

1 東京の 人口は ニューヨークの 人口より （多い。少ない。）
2 日本では 8月が いちばん （暑い。寒い。）
3 富士山は マッターホルンより （高い。低い。）
4 ひらがなは 漢字より （新しい。古い。）
5 日本の 新幹線は フランスの 新幹線より （速い。遅い。）
6 まぐろは たいより （大きい。小さい）
7 2月と 3月と 4月の 中で 3月が いちばん （長い。短い。）

VOCABULARY

- だれ who
- どこ where
- 行(い)きました went
- 何(なに、なん) what
- 東京(とうきょう) Tokyo
- 人口(じんこう) population
- ニューヨーク New York
- 多(おお)い many, much
- 少(すく)ない few, little
- 日本(にほん、にっぽん)で in Japan
- 8月(はちがつ) August
- 暑(あつ)い hot
- 寒(さむ)い cold
- 富士山(ふじさん) Mt. Fuji
- マッターホルン Mt. Matterhorn
- 高(たか)い high, tall
- 低(ひく)い low, short
- ひらがな hiragana [writing script]
- 漢字(かんじ) kanji, Chinese characters
- 新(あたら)しい new
- 古(ふる)い old
- 新幹線(しんかんせん) the Shinkansen super express train
- フランス France
- 速(はや)い fast, rapid
- 遅(おそ)い slow, late
- まぐろ tuna
- たい sea bream
- 大(おお)きい big
- 小(ちい)さい small
- 2月(にがつ) February
- 3月(さんがつ) March
- 4月(しがつ) April
- 中(なか)で among
- 長(なが)い long
- 短(みじか)い short

TASKS

1. 魚つり
Gone fishing

明子さんと まさみさんと 信子さんと ゆみさんが 川へ 魚つりに 行きました。

Akiko, Masami, Nobuko, and Yumi went to the river to fish. Look at the picture and answer the following questions.

明子さん　　まさみさん　　信子さん　　ゆみさん

【質問】

1　まさみさんと ゆみさんと どちらが 背が 高いですか。
2　だれが いちばん 背が 低いですか。
3　明子さんと まさみさんと どちらの かみが 長いですか。
4　魚の 数は だれが いちばん 少ないですか。
5　魚を いちばん 多く つった 人は 何匹 つりましたか。

VOCABULARY

- 明子(あきこ)、まさみ、信子(のぶこ)、ゆみ are all common given names and さん is a polite suffix.
- 川(かわ)　river
- に　for: here, particle to indicate purpose
- 行(い)きました　went
- 質問(しつもん)　question
- 背(せ)　height
- か　question particle
- だれ　who
- かみ　hair
- 長(なが)い　long
- 数(かず)　number
- 多(おお)く　many, much
- つった　caught, fished
- 人(ひと)　person
- 何匹(なんびき)　how many: 匹(ひき、びき、ぴき) is a counter for small animals including fish
- つりました　caught, fished

2. 同窓会
Class reunion

山中さんと 川田さんと 青木さんと 小林さんが 高校の 同窓会で 同じ テーブルに すわりました。

Yamanaka, Kawada, Aoki, and Kobayashi were sitting at the same table at a recent high-school reunion dinner. Read the six sentences below and compete the missing information from the chart.

1. 小林さんは 29歳で、山中さんより 1歳 年上です。
2. 青木さんは 小林さんより 1歳 年上で、川田さんは 小林さんより 2歳 年下です。
3. 川田さんは 自宅に 住んで いて、家賃は 払って いません。今、働いていません。
4. 青木さんは 毎朝 通勤に 2時間 かかります。寮に 住んで いて、毎月 3万円 払います。
5. 山中さんは 青木さんの 半分の 時間で 会社へ 行けます。家賃は 5万円です。
6. 小林さんの 家賃は 青木さんの 家賃の 2倍です。通勤に 山中さんの 3倍の 時間が かかります。

下の 表に 数字を 入れなさい。

	山中	川田	青木	小林
年齢	(1) 歳	(2) 歳	(3) 歳	(4) 歳
家賃	(5) 円	(6) 円	(7) 円	(8) 円
通勤時間	(9) 時間	(10) 時間	(11) 時間	(12) 時間

VOCABULARY

- 山中（やまなか）、川田（かわだ）、青木（あおき）、小林（こばやし） are all common family names.
- 高校（こうこう） high school
- で in, at, on
- 同（おな）じ same
- テーブル table
- ～に すわりました sat on/in
- ～歳（さい） ～ years old: a counter for age
- で being
- 年上（としうえ） older
- 年下（としした） younger
- 自宅（じたく） one's home
- 住（す）んで いて living
- 家賃（やちん） rent
- 払（はら）って いません is not paying
- 今（いま） now, at present
- 働（はたら）いて いません is not working, doesn't have a job
- 毎朝（まいあさ） every morning
- 通勤（つうきん）に for commuting
- 時間（じかん） hour, time
- かかります to take, to spend
- 寮（りょう） dormitory
- 毎月（まいつき） every month
- 3万円（さんまんえん） ¥30,000
- 払（はら）います to pay
- 半分（はんぶん） half
- 行（い）けます can go
- 2倍（にばい） double, twice as much
- 3倍（さんばい） three times as much
- 下（した） below
- 表（ひょう）に in the chart
- 数字（すうじ） number
- 入（い）れなさい put (in): an imperative form
- 年齢（ねんれい） age

6 もしもし **Hello.**

DIALOGUE

1. パテルさんが もうすぐ インドへ 帰る。林さんは パテルさんの お別れパーティーを 開こうと 思っている。そこで、佐藤さんに 電話を かけた。リーーン

2. もしもし、佐藤で ございます。

3. もしもし、わたし 林ですが、ご主人 いらっしゃいますか。

はい、少々 お待ち くださいませ。

4. もしもし、佐藤です。

あ、佐藤さん。ぼく 林です。こんばんは。

5. じつは、パテルさんが 今度 国へ 帰るそうです。

ええっ、パテルさんが インドへ？ いつ？

VOCABULARY

- パテルさん Ms. Patel
- もうすぐ soon
- インド India
- へ to
- 帰る to return
- 林さん Mr. Lin
- は as for, speaking of
- の of
- お別れパーティー farewell party
- 開こう to intend to hold/open
- と that
- 思って いる is thinking, to think
- そこで then
- 佐藤さん Mr. Sato
- に to
- 電話を かけた made a phone call
- リーン sound of telephone ringing
- もしもし hello
- で ございます is, are, am
- わたし I
- です is, are, am
- が [weak] but
- ご主人 [someone's] husband
- いらっしゃいます is, to exist
- か question particle
- はい yes
- 少々 a minute, a little
- お待ち くださいませ please wait
- あ Oh!
- ぼく [masculine] I
- こんばんは Good evening
- じつは the fact is, to be frank with you
- 今度 shortly, soon

OBJECTIVES:
Using very polite Japanese, introducing conjunctions and speaking on the telephone.

- 国 [one's] country
- ～そうです I hear, they say
- ええっ Oh! What!
- いつ when
- 9月10日 September 10th
- だ is, are, am
- だから so, therefore
- みんなで [all] together
- 思う to think
- そうだ That's a good idea, That's right
- ね isn't it?
- 8月 August
- 終わり end
- いい good
- 26日 26th
- 土曜日 Saturday
- か or
- 27日 27th
- 日曜日 Sunday
- どう how
- かな wonder
- ほう alternative
- 思います to think
- そうか Is that so? OK
- じゃあ then
- さて well, now
- どこ where
- で at, in, on
- やろう to intend to hold/do

CULTURE

Soobetsukai and Kangeikai

Soobetsukai and *kangeikai* are regular events on the business calendar. Whenever an employee retires or is transferred to another part of the organization, colleagues will throw a *soobetsukai* leaving party to say thank you and good-bye. Newcomers to a company or department will similarly be welcomed by their new colleagues and boss with a *kangeikai* Traditionally, the *soobetsukai* was also a special gathering of friends and relatives to see someone off on a long journey, especially to a foreign destination. However, in today's age of frequent overseas travel, these good-bye bashes are reserved for foreign postings or studies abroad. At both the *soobetsukai* and the *kangeikai*, a speech is expected from the person concerned and a toast is drunk by all. Musical entertainment is rare but food is plentiful and often served buffet-style so people can circulate. After the main party is over, smaller and more intimate groups often sneak off to a favorite bar for a *nijikai* or second part of the party.

PRONUNCIATION

Listen to the tape and repeat. High pitches are marked with ⌈ and low pitches with ⌉. All words appearing in **bold** should be stressed. Note that hyphenated phrases are treated as one word.

1. Pateru-san-ga moosugu **Indo**-e kaeru. Rin-san-wa Pateru-san-no **o-wakare-paatii**-o hirakoo-to omotte-iru. Sokode, Satoo-san-ni **denwa**-o kaketa.

2. Moshi-moshi, Satoo-de gozaimasu.

3. Moshi-moshi, watashi Rin-desu-ga, **go-shujin** irasshaimasu-ka.

   Hai, **shooshoo** o-machi kudasai-mase.

4. Moshi-moshi, **Satoo**-desu.

   A, Satoo-san. Boku **Rin**-desu. Kombanwa.

5. Jitsuwa, Pateru-san-ga kondo kuni-e **kaeru**-soo-desu.

   Ee, Pateru-san-ga **Indo**-e? Itsu?

6. **Ku-gatsu-too-ka**-da-soo-desu. Dakara, minnade **o-wakarepaatii**-o hirakoo-to omoo-no-desu-ga.

7. Soo-da-ne. Hachi-gatsu-no **owari**-ga ii-ne. Ni-juu-roku-nichi-no **do-yoobi**-ka ni-juu-shichi-nichi-no **nichi-yoobi**-wa doo-ka-na.

8. **Do-yoobi**-no hoo-ga ii-to omoimasu.

9. Soo-ka. Jaa **ni-juu-roku-nichi**-da. Sate, **doko**-de yaroo-ka.

NOTES

1 パテルさんが もうすぐ インドへ 帰る。林さんは パテルさんの お別れパーティーを 開こうと 思って いる。そこで、佐藤さんに 電話を かけた。
Ms. Patel will soon return home to India. Mr. Lin plans to have a farewell party for Ms. Patel so he has called Mr. Sato.

❶ が is a particle that introduces the subject of the verb.

❷ へ is a particle that here shows physical direction.

❸ は is a particle to introduce the topic. (See Notes to Module 1.)

❹ の is a particle that indicates the noun which modifies the one after it.

❺ を is the direct object particle.

❻ 開こう is the [y]oo form of the verb 開く (to hold a function, to open.) (See Notes in Module 4.)

❼ と is a particle that marks somebody's words or thoughts like a quotation mark.

❽ 思って いる The て／で-form of the verb plus いる (plain) or います (polite) indicates a continuing action or state. (See Notes in Vocabulary on p.56)

❾ に is used as a direction particle, indicating to whom the action of one's verb is directed.

❿ 電話を かけた is the plain past form of the verb 電話を かける.

2 もしもし、佐藤で ございます。
Hello, Sato residence.

❶ もしもし is used as a telephone greeting like "hello."

❷ で ございます is the most polite form of the copula.

3 もしもし、わたし 林ですが、ご主人 いらっしゃいますか。
――はい、少々 お待ち くださいませ。
Hello, my name is Lin. Is your husband at home? – Yes, just a moment, please.

❶ 少々 お待ち くださいませ Each word here is in its most polite form:
　　少々－ちょっと　　お待ち－待って　　くださいませ－ください

❷ です is a polite form of the copula, but not as polite as で ございます.

❸ が is used here as a conjunction that joins the two sentences, but does not have a special meaning. However, as a conjunction, が often connects two contrasting sentences:
　　パテルさんは 国へ 帰るが、私は 帰らない。Ms. Patel is going back to her country, but I am not.

❹ いらっしゃいます is the honorific form of いる. (See Notes in Module 2 for verbs of existence.) いる or the more polite forms います and いらっしゃいます are often used to show somebody's location.

❺ か is a particle that acts like a question mark.

4 もしもし、佐藤です。——あ、佐藤さん。ぼく 林です。こんばんは。
Hello, this is Sato. – Oh, Mr. Sato. This is Lin. Good evening.

あ is an exclamation like "oh."

5 じつは、パテルさんが 今度 国へ 帰るそうです。——ええっ、パテルさんが インドへ？ いつ？
I hear Ms. Patel will be returning to India soon. – What? Ms. Patel is returning to India? When?

そうです is the polite form of そうだ.
When attached to the plain form (here, 帰る), -そうだ or -そうです suggests the speaker is reporting something they have heard, read, etc. Even if the statement is not actual hearsay, it is useful to use when you are not sure of something yourself.

6 9月 10日だそうです。だから、みんなで お別れパーティーを 開こうと 思うのですが。
September 10th, I hear. So, I thought we could have a farewell party.

❶ -のです is the polite form of -のだ, which gives sentences a colloquial, emphatic, or explanatory flavor. (See **2**-❸ in Notes to Module 4.)

❷ が is a conjunction, often used after a suggestion, to imply that the speaker wishes to hear the other person's opinion. It is very common in Japanese to use が to imply something that is not actually said. (See **2**-❹ in Notes to Module 4.)

7 そうだね。8月の 終わりが いいね。26日の 土曜日か 27日の 日曜日は どうかな。
That's a good idea. I think the end of August would be fine. How about Saturday 26th or Sunday 27th?

❶ ね is a particle used when the speaker is seeking confirmation.
❷ いい is an い-adjective.
❸ 土曜日か　か here means "or."
❹ どう means how; used with かな, a form used by men, it means "how about...?"

8 土曜日の ほうが いいと 思います。
I think Saturday would be better.

❶ ほう is used optionally in sentences of comparision. (See Notes to Module 5.)
❷ 思います is the polite form of 思う.

9 そうか。じゃあ 26日だ。さて、どこで やろうか。
Okay. It's the 26th then. Well, where should we have the party?

❶ で is a particle indicating where the action of a verb takes place. (See Notes to Module 2.)
❷ やろう is the [y]oo form of やる and indicates intention "to hold or do something."

DRILLS

1. 質問に 答えなさい。
Answer the following questions.

1 だれが いつ インドへ 帰りますか。
  → (   )が (   )に インドへ 帰ります。

2 林さんは だれに 電話を かけましたか。
  → (   )に 電話を かけました。

3 いつ お別れパーティーを 開きますか。
  → (   )です。

4 お別れパーティーは 土曜日ですか、日曜日ですか。
  → (   )です。

2. 下の 語を 使って、文を 完成させなさい。
Using the words below, complete the passage by filling in the blanks.

林さんは 日本語の 歌が 大好きだ。そこで、わたしは いっしょに カラオケパーティーを (1   ) と 思って、林さんと 友だちに 電話を (2   )。友だちは いつでも いいそうだが、林さんは 今週 いそがしい (3   ) だ。だから、カラオケパーティーは 来週の 週末に しようと (4   )。

カラオケは 今 外国でも 人気が (5   )。林さんは 中国語の 歌も (6   ) そうだ。林さんの 中国語の カラオケも (7   ) たい。

[思う した じょうずだ しよう ある そう 聞き]

VOCABULARY

- だれ who
- 帰(かえ)ります to return [home]
- 電話(でんわ)を かけました made a phone call
- 開(ひら)きます to hold, to open
- 林(りん)さん Mr. Lin
- 日本語(にほんご) Japanese language
- 歌(うた) song
- 大好(だいす)き to like very much
- そこで so, then
- いっしょに together
- カラオケ karaoke music
- しよう to intend to hold/do
- 友(とも)だち friend
- 電話(でんわ)を した made a phone call
- いつでも any time, whenever
- 今週(こんしゅう) this week
- いそがしい busy
- 来週(らいしゅう) next week
- 週末(しゅうまつ) weekend
- 今(いま) now
- 外国(がいこく)でも even in foreign countries
- 人気(にんき)がある to be popular
- 中国語(ちゅうごくご) Chinese language
- じょうず to be good at
- 聞(き)きたい to want to listen to

TASKS

1. だれが どの いすに すわって いるか。
Who is sitting in which chair?

ここは パーティー会場です。佐藤さんの テーブルに 王さん、パテルさん、林さん、スミスさん、キムさんが います。だれが どの いすに すわって いますか。

At the party, Mr. Wang, Ms. Patel, Mr. Lin, Ms. Smith, and Ms. Kim all sat at the same table as Mr. Sato. But who was sitting in which chair?

1　佐藤さんは **(A)**の いすに すわって います。
2　佐藤さんの 右に キムさんが います。
3　キムさんの 前に スミスさんが います。
4　佐藤さんと スミスさんの あいだに 林さんが います。
5　林さんの 前に 王さんが います。
6　パテルさんは あいて いる いすに すわりました。

(A)　佐藤さん
(B)　＿＿＿さん
(C)　＿＿＿さん
(D)　＿＿＿さん
(E)　＿＿＿さん
(F)　＿＿＿さん

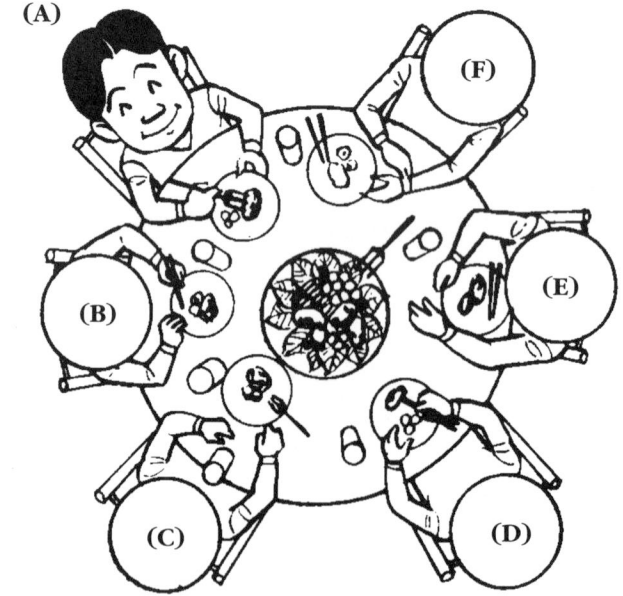

VOCABULARY
- ここ here, this place
- パーティー party
- 会場(かいじょう) place, site
- テーブル table
- 王(おう)さん Mr. Wang
- います there is, to exist
- だれ who
- どの いす which chair
- すわって います is sitting
- 右(みぎ) the right
- 前(まえ) front
- ～と～の あいだ between ～ and ～
- あいて いる to be empty
- すわりました sat

NOTES
The て/で-form of the verb plus いる (plain) or います (polite) indicates a continuing action or state.
いすに すわって いる／います
to be sitting in a chair
ビールを 飲んで いる／います
to be drinking beer
カバンを 持って いる／います
to have/be carrying a bag
あいて いる (to be empty) added to the noun いす(chair) means "empty chair."

2. みどりさんの 家は どれ？
Which one is Midori's house?

正夫さんは みどりさんの 家を 探して いますが、まだ 見つかりません。
そこで みどりさんに 電話を かけました。
次の 電話の 会話を 読んで、みどりさんの 家を いっしょに 探して ください。

Masao is trying to find Midori's house, but has gotten lost. So, he decided to give her a call. Read their telephone conversation below and help Masao find Midori's house.

みどり：もしもし、あ、正夫さん、どう したの？ みんな 待って いるのよ。
正夫：　近くまで 来て いると 思うけど… 家の 前に 大きな 木が ある？
みどり：ええ、あるわ。太郎さんが 車で 来て、家の 前に 車が 止めて あるわ。
正夫：　木は 家に 向かって 右側？ それとも 左側？
みどり：ええっと、向かって 左側。そうそう、家は 2階建てよ。

VOCABULARY

- 正夫（まさお）　a given name
- 探（さが）して います　is looking for
- が　but
- まだ　yet, still
- 見（み）つかりません　cannot be found
- 〜に 電話（でんわ）を かけました　called 〜
- 次（つぎ）　following, next
- 読（よ）んで　reading
- いっしょに　together
- 探（さが）して ください　please look for
- どう したの　What happened to you? どう [how] + した[did] + の[here, a question particle]
- みんな　all
- 待（ま）って いる　is waiting
- のよ　you know: particle for emphasis, used by a female speaker
- まで　as far as
- 来（き）て いる　have come
- 〜と 思（おも）う　to think that
- けど　[weak, colloquial] but
- 前（まえ）　front
- に　in, at, on
- 大（おお）きな　big
- 木（き）　tree
- ある　there is, to exist
- わ　particle used by a female speaker to express her weak assertion or volition
- 車（くるま）　car
- で　by
- 来（き）て　coming
- 止（と）めて ある　is stopped, is parked
- 〜に 向（む）かって　facing, toward 〜
- 右側（みぎがわ）　right-hand side
- それとも　or
- 左側（ひだりがわ）　left-hand side
- ええっと　well, er, let me see
- そうそう　Oh, yes!
- 2階建（にかいだ）て　two-story [house]
- よ　you know: particle attached to a noun and used by a female speaker for emphasis

7 ごしゅうしょうさまです

You have my sympathies.

DIALOGUE

1 キムさんが デパートで 佐藤夫人に 会った。

2 あ、佐藤さん、こんにちは。
お父さまが 先日 おなくなりに なったそうですね。

3 ごしゅうしょうさまで ございます。
ぺこ
どうも ありがとう ございます。

VOCABULARY

- キムさん Ms. Kim
- デパート department store
- で at, in, on
- 佐藤夫人 Mrs. Sato
- 会った met
- あ Oh!
- こんにちは Hello, Good afternoon
- お父さま [someone's] father
- お亡くなりに なった died, passed away
- 〜そうです I hear, They say
- ね isn't it?
- ごしゅうしょうさまで ございます You have my sympathies, Please accept my condolences
- どうも very, much
- ありがとう ございます Thank you
- ぺこ sound-effect word for a bow
- ご病気 sickness, illness
- だった was, were
- いいえ no
- 元気 fine, high-spirited
- でした was, were
- が but
- 突然 suddenly
- のういっけつ apoplexy, hemorrhage
- で with, owing to
- たおれました collapsed, fell ill

OBJECTIVES:
Using honorific Japanese and expressing your sympathies.

4　ご病気だったのですか。
　　いいえ、元気でしたが、突然のういっけつでたおれました。

5　そうでしたか。おさびしくなりましたね。

6　はい、まだ慣れなくて、今朝もごはんに呼びに行って…

7　そうでしょうね。お体に気をつけてください。

8　ごていねいにありがとうございます。

- そうでしたか　Is that so? Really?
- おさびしく　lonely
- なりました　became
- はい　yes
- まだ　yet, still
- 慣れなくて　being not used to
- 今朝　this morning
- も　also
- ごはんに　for meal
- 呼び　calling
- 行って　going
- そうでしょうね　I understand, That must be the case
- お体　health, body
- 〜に 気を つけて ください　please take care of 〜
- ごていねいに　being polite

7 ごしゅうしょうさまです …… 59

CULTURE

Funerals

Funerals in Japan, like weddings, are often costly affairs for both attendants and organizers, since mourners are expected to present the bereaved family with a cash gift in a special envelope and the family must reciprocate accordingly at a later date. Unlike the Shinto and often pseudo-Christian weddings however, most Japanese funerals follow Buddhist dictates. On the evening following the death, the family stay up all night with the body in a room decorated with lanterns and a large, framed photograph of the deceased. At this time, friends, relatives, and business associates call by to pay their respects. After cremation the following day, mourners gather to offer burning incense to the fire. Special salt is provided for purifying the pollution of death. There is a strict, black dress code, but the large wreaths outside the house are in the Buddhist mourning colors of yellow, blue, and green.

PRONUNCIATION

Listen to the tape and repeat. High pitches are marked with ⌈ and low pitches with ⌉. All words appearing in **bold** should be stressed. Note that hyphenated phrases are treated as one word.

1. Kimu-san-ga depaato-de **Satoo-fujin**-ni atta.

2. A, Satoo-san, **konnichiwa**. O-too-sama-ga senjitsu **o-nakunari**-ni natta-soo-desu-ne.

3. **Go-shuushoo-sama**-de gozaimasu.

   Doomo **arigatoo** gozaimasu.

4. **Go-byooki**-datta-no-desu-ka.

   Iie, genki-deshita-ga, totsuzen **nooikketsu**-de taoremashita.

5. Soo-deshita-ka. **O-sabishiku** narimashita-ne.

6. Hai, mada narenakute, kesa-mo **gohan**-ni yobi-ni itte...

7. Soo-deshoo-ne. **O-karada**-ni ki-o tsukete kudasai.

8. Go-teenee-ni **arigatoo** gozaimasu.

NOTES

1 キムさんが デパートで 佐藤夫人に 会った。
Ms. Kim met Mrs. Sato in a department store.

❶ が is a particle indicating the subject of a verb.

❷ で is a particle that, here, marks the location where the action of a verb takes place.

❸ に 会った is the past tense of (somebody) に 会う, "to meet someone."

2 あ、佐藤さん、こんにちは。お父さまが 先日 おなくなりに なったそうですね。
Hello, Mrs. Sato. I heard your father passed away the other day.

❶ お父さま is the honorific form of お父さん.

❷ おなくなりに なった is the honorific past form of the verb なくなる.
When the speaker wants to show utmost respect for another person, the subject of the sentence, he or she will use so-called honorific forms of verbs, nouns, and adjectives pertaining to that person.

Honorific verb forms (in descending order of politeness):
i) お(the bound form) に なる／なります (the the bound form of a verb is formed by dropping the -ます ending)　飲む―お飲みに なる／なります (to drink)
ii) Verb stem + (r) are - ru/masu　飲む―飲まれる／(飲まれ)ます
Remember that the polite ます[or です] form is used when the speaker is expected to be polite to the listener.

Some honorific verb forms have to be memorized:
i) いらっしゃる／いらっしゃいます— used to mean いる(to exist, be), 行く(to go), and 来る(to come)　ii) おっしゃる／おっしゃいます—言う (to say)　iii) なさる／なさいます—する (to do)
iv) ごらんになる―見る (to see, look at)

Honorific nouns and adjectives:
The honorific forms of nouns and adjectives are made by adding the prefix お or ご. There is no hard and fast rule, but in general お is attached to words of Japanese origin and ご to kanji compounds.

お手紙— letter　　ご研究— research　　お忙しい— busy　　ご親切— kind

ご病気だったのですか。(See **4**.)

おさびしく なりましたね。(See **5**.)

お体に 気を つけて ください。(See **7**.)

ごていねいに ありがとう ございます。(See **8**.)

❸ そうです is the polite form of そうだ。(See **5** in Notes to Module 6.)

❹ ね is a particle that here indicates the speaker is confirming something.

3 ごしゅうしょうさまで ございます。――どうも ありがとう ございます。
You have my deepest sympathies.– Thank you very much.

で ございます is the most polite form of the copula.

4 ご病気 だったのですか。——いいえ、元気でしたが、突然 のういっけつで たおれました。
Had he been sick? – No, he was very healthy, but he suddenly collapsed with cerebral hemorrhaging.

❶ だった is the plain past form of the copula.

❷ ご病気だったのですか。 The addition of のです, often used to mark an explanation, gives the question the literal feel of the English "Was it that he had been sick?" (See **2**-❸ in Notes to Module 4.)

❸ か is a particle that functions like a question mark.

❹ 元気 is a な-adjective.

❺ でした is the polite past form of the copula.

❻ が is a conjuction that here joins the two sentences. (See **3**-❸ in Notes to Module 6.)

❼ で is a particle, that here, marks the cause for the action of the verb that follows.

❽ たおれました is the polite past form of the verb たおれる.

5 そうでしたか。おさびしく なりましたね。
Really? I am sure you must be quite lonely.

❶ おさびしく is an honorific of さびしい in its adverbial form.

❷ なりました is the polite past tense of the verb なる.

6 はい、まだ 慣れなくて、今朝も ごはんに 呼びに 行って…
Yes. I'm not used to it yet. I even went to call him for breakfast this morning.

❶ 慣れなくて is the て-form of the negative of 慣れる, 慣れない.

❷ も is a particle meaning "also."

❸ に is a particle that marks purpose.

❹ 呼び is the bound form of the verb 呼ぶ.

❺ 行って is the て-form of the verb 行く.

7 そうでしょうね。お体に 気を つけて ください。
I understand. Please take care of yourself.

❶ お体 is an honorific form of 体.

❷ 気を つけて ください is the polite request form of the verb 気を つける.

8 ごていねいに ありがとう ございます。
Thank you very much.

ごていねいに is an honorific adverbial form of the な-adjective ていねい.

DRILLS

1. 質問に 答えなさい。
Answer the following questions.

1 キムさんは どこで 佐藤夫人に 会いましたか。
 → (　　　　　)で 会いました。

2 だれの お父さんが なくなりましたか。
 → (　　　　　)の お父さんです。

3 佐藤夫人の お父さんは ずっと 病気でしたか。
 → いいえ、元気でしたが、突然 (　　　　　)で たおれました。

2. 番号の ついた 語を 敬語に 変えて、文章を 完成させなさい。
Complete the passage, putting the numbered words into their honorific forms.

先日 小学校時代の 鈴木先生から（**1** 手紙）→（　　　　　）を いただいた。鈴木先生は もうすぐ70歳に（**2** なる）→（　　　　　）。（**3** 忙しい）→（　　　　　）そうだが、たいへん（**4** 元気）→（　　　　　）で、今も 毎日（**5** 好き）→（　　　　　）な（**6** 酒）→（　　　　　）を（**7** 飲む）→（　　　　　）そうだ。テレビの 時代劇も よく（**8** 見る）→（　　　　　）そうだ。

VOCABULARY		
●どこ where	●鈴木先生（すずきせんせい） Professor/Mr. Suzuki	●たいへん very
●会(あ)いました met	●から from	●元気(げんき)で being healthy
●だれ who	●手紙(てがみ) letter	●今(いま) now
●の of	●を particle indicating the direct object	●毎日(まいにち) every day
●お父(とう)さん [someone's] father	●いただいた received	●好(す)き to like, to be fond of
●なくなりました died, passed away	●もうすぐ soon	●酒(さけ) sake, alchoholic beverage
●は as for, speaking of	●〜歳(さい) 〜 years old	●飲(の)む to drink
●ずっと all the time, all this while	●〜に なる to become, to turn 〜	●テレビ TV, television
●病気(びょうき) sickness, illness	●忙(いそが)しい busy	●時代劇(じだいげき) samurai drama
●小学校時代(しょうがっこうじだい) elementary school days	●〜そうだ I hear, They say 〜	●よく often
		●見(み)る to watch, to see

TASKS

1. どの あいさつが どの 場面の あいさつか。
Which greeting is used in which situation?

下に 七つの あいさつが あります。それぞれの あいさつは どの 場面の あいさつでしょうか。

Below are seven different greetings that are used in completely different situations. Match the correct greeting (numbered **1-7**) with right situation (labeled **a** to **g**.)

《あいさつ》 《場面》

1 お帰りなさい。 Welcome home. ( )
2 ご入学 おめでとう ございます。 Congratulations! (on your admission [to school]) ( )
3 ごしゅうしょうさまで ございます。 Please accept my condolences. ( )
4 気を つけて、行って らっしゃい。 Take care and goodbye. ( )
5 それは いけませんね。どうぞ お大事に。 That's too bad. Please take good care of [him]. ( )
6 残念でしたね。 That was too bad. ( )
7 きのうは ごちそうさまでした。 I really enjoyed the meal yesterday. ( )

《場面》

a 山田君は 朝 7時半に 学校へ 行きます。お母さんが 山田君に こう 言います。
b 吉田さんは 試験に 受かりませんでした。友だちが 吉田さんに こう 言います。
c 青木さんの お母さんが 亡くなりました。友だちが 青木さんに こう 言います。
d クラークさんは 和子さんの うちで、晩ごはんを ごちそうに なりました。次の 日に クラークさんは 和子さんに こう 言います。
e 木下さんの お父さんが 入院しました。そのことを 聞いて、中川さんが 木下さんに こう 言います。
f 田中さんが 学校から 帰って きました。お母さんが 田中さんに こう 言います。
g 小川君が 大学に 入りました。となりの おばさんが 小川君に こう 言います。

VOCABULARY

- 下(した)に below
- 七(なな)つ seven
- あいさつ greeting
- あります there is, to exist
- それぞれ each
- どの which
- 場面(ばめん) situation
- でしょう will probably be
- 山田(やまだ)、吉田(よしだ)、青木(あおき)、クラーク(Clark)、木下(きのした)、中川(なかがわ)、田中(たなか)、小川(おがわ) are all family names. 和子(かずこ) is a given name.
- 君(くん) a masculine suffix used for boys
- 朝(あさ) [in the] morning, A.M.
- 7時半(しちじはん) seven-thirty
- 学校(がっこう) school
- 行(い)きます to go
- お母(かあ)さん [someone's] mother
- こう like this, this way
- 言(い)います to say
- 試験(しけん) test, examination
- 受(う)かりませんでした didn't pass
- 友(とも)だち friend[s]
- 亡(な)くなりました died, passed away
- うち home, house
- 晩(ばん)ごはん supper, dinner
- ごちそうに なりました was offered a feast
- 次(つぎ)の 日(ひ) the next day
- お父(とう)さん [someone's] father
- 入院(にゅういん)しました was hospitalized
- その こと that thing / news
- 聞(き)いて hearing, listening
- から from
- 帰(かえ)って きました came back
- 大学(だいがく) college, university
- 入(はい)りました entered
- となり neighbor, neighboring
- おばさん lady, aunt

7 ごしゅうしょうさまです

2. パテルさんの くつ
Ms. Patel's shoes

パテルさんが くつを 買いました。
次の 文を 並べかえて、一つの 話を 作って ください。

Rearrange the following sentences **A** to **G** and make a story about Ms. Patel's shoes.

A パテルさんは 日本の くつの サイズが わかりません。だから、「足を はかって ください。」と 言いました。

B パテルさんが 友だちと くつ屋へ 行きました。店の 人が 出て きました。

C 「あの ショーウィンドーの 中の 茶色の くつを 見せて ください。」と パテルさんが 言いました。

D 店の 人が 「これが あの 茶色の くつの サイズ23です。」と 言って、くつを 持って きました。

E 「いらっしゃいませ。どんな くつが よろしいでしょうか。」と 店の 人が 言いました。

F 「お客さまの くつの サイズは？」と くつ屋さんが 聞きました。

G くつ屋さんは パテルさんの 足を はかって、「お客さまの サイズは 23ですね。」と 言いました。

VOCABULARY

- パテルさん Ms. Patel
- くつ shoes
- 買(か)いました bought
- 次(つぎ) next, following
- 文(ぶん) sentence
- 並(なら)べかえて rearranging
- 一(ひと)つ one
- 話(はなし) story, talk
- 作(つく)って ください please make
- 日本(にほん、にっぽん) Japan
- サイズ size
- わかりません not to know, not to understand
- だから therefore
- 足(あし) foot
- はかって ください please measure
- ～と 言(い)いました said [that] ～
- 友(とも)だちと with a friend
- くつ屋(や) shoe store
- へ to
- 行(い)きました went
- 店(みせ)の 人(ひと) store clerk
- 出(で)て きました came out, appeared
- ショーウィンドー show window
- 中(なか) inside
- 茶色(ちゃいろ) light brown
- 見(み)せて ください please show
- これ this one
- あの that __ over there
- 言(い)って saying
- 持(も)って きました brought
- いらっしゃいませ May I help you?
- どんな what kind of
- よろしい good
- お客(きゃく)さま customer, guest
- くつ屋(や)さん shoemaker
- 聞(き)きました asked
- はかって measuring

8 どちらまで

Where to?

DIALOGUE

1 スミスさんは終電車に乗り遅れた。それで、タクシーを利用して、うちへ帰ることにした。

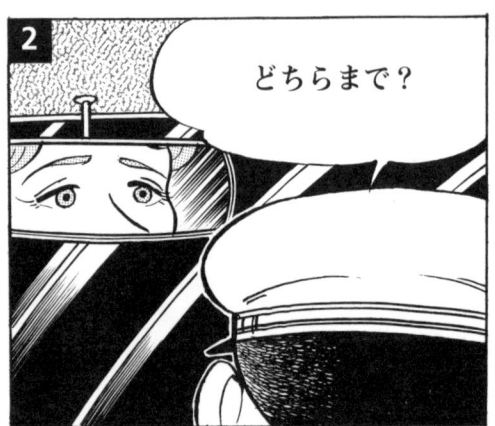

2 どちらまで？

3 東武東上線の大山駅の方へ行ってください。

大山駅ですね。

4 次の角を右に曲がってください。

それから、あのガソリンスタンドを左に行ってください。

VOCABULARY

- スミスさん Ms. Smith
- は as for, speaking of
- 終電車 last train
- に for
- 乗り遅れた missed [the train]
- それで then
- タクシー taxi
- 利用して using
- うち home
- へ to
- 帰る to return [home]
- ことにした decided to
- ○キーッ sound of brakes screeching
- どちら where
- まで as far as, until
- 東武東上線 the Tobu-tojo line
- の of
- 大山駅 Oyama Station
- 方 direction
- 行ってください please go
- です is, are, am
- ね isn't it?
- ○ブローッ sound of car pulling away
- 次 next
- 角 corner
- 右 right
- に to

OBJECTIVES:
Using demonstratives and giving directions.

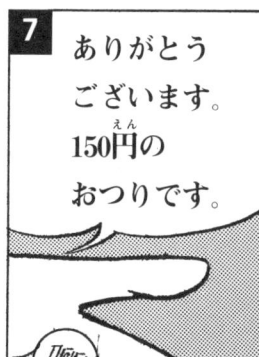

- 曲がって ください please turn
- それから [and] then
- あの that _ over there
- ガソリンスタンド gas station
- 左 left
- その that _
- おすしやさん sushi shop
- 前 front
- で at, in, on
- 止めて ください please stop
- 円 yen
- これで with this
- お願いします please [take]
- ありがとう ございます thank you
- おつり change
- あ Oh! Ah!
- お客さん passenger, guest
- 忘れもの a thing left behind
- よ you know
- そうだ That's right! Oh!
- 雑誌 magazine
- 忘れる to forget
- ところだった was about to, almost
- どうも very, much
- すみません Thank you, I'm sorry
- ありがとう ございました
  Thank you [for what you did]

CULTURE

Using Taxis

The typical Japanese cab is a large four-door sedan powered by a diesel engine through manual transmission. The cabbie, often wearing a peaked cap and spotless white driving gloves is able to open and close the rear doors automatically from the comfort of the driver's seat. Finding a taxi, day and night, is relatively straightforward: Simply hail a cab displaying a red vacant light, or wait in line at a taxi stand near a station or hotel. But don't expect the cabbie to know exactly how to get to where you want to go. The city streets of Tokyo form a complicated maze of narrow paths that can confuse even the most experienced drivers. Be prepared to explain the quickest and most convenient route to your destination or better still, take along a map. Remember, as with restaurants and barbers, tipping is not common in Japan. Many taxis are fitted with a cellular phone and TV, and all cabs are air-conditioned.

PRONUNCIATION

Listen to the tape and repeat. High pitches are marked with ⌐ and low pitches with ⌐. All words appearing in **bold** should be stressed. Note that hyphenated phrases are treated as one word.

1. Sumisu-san wa **shuudensha**-ni nori-okureta. Sorede, **takushii**-o riyooshite, uchi-e kaeru koto-ni shita.

2. Dochira-made?

3. Toobu-toojoo-sen-no **Ooyama-eki**-no hoo-e itte kudasai.

   Ooyama-eki-desu-ne.

4. Tsugi-no kado-o **migi**-ni magatte kudasai...Sorekara, ano gasorin-sutando-o **hidari**-ni itte kudasai.

5. Sono **o-sushiya-san**-no mae-de tomete kudasai.

6. Ni-sen-hap-pyaku-go-juu-en-desu.

   Kore-de onegaishimasu.

7. **Arigatoo** gozaimasu. **Hyaku-go-juu-en**-no otsuri-desu.

8. A, o-kyaku-san. Wasuremono-desu-yo.

9. Soo-da. **Zasshi**-o wasureru tokoro-datta. Doomo **sumimasen**.

   Arigatoo gozaimashita.

NOTES

1 スミスさんは 終電車に 乗り遅れた。
それで、タクシーを 利用して、うちへ 帰る ことに した。
Ms. Smith missed the last train. So she then decided to take a taxi home.

❶ は is a particle that here introduces the topic of the sentence. (See **1** in Notes to Module 1.)

❷ に is used to mark the mode of transport used with the verb 乗る (to get on, to ride.) Here, it indicates the mode of transport missed when used with 乗り遅れた.

❸ 乗り遅れた is the plain past form of 乗り遅れる.

❹ を is the direct object particle here.

❺ 利用して is the て-form of 利用する. Used this way to connect the clauses, the て-form corresponds to "-ing."

❻ へ is a particle that here shows physical direction.

❼ ことに した is the plain past form of (plain verb) + ことに する (to decide to do something.)

2 どちらまで。
Where to?

❶ どちら is the polite form of どこ (where.)

❷ まで here marks the limit of a physical distance.

3 東武東上線の 大山駅の 方へ 行って ください。— 大山駅ですね。
Please go in the direction of Oyama Station on the Tobu-tojo line. – Oyama Station, right?

❶ の is a particle that here marks the noun modifying the following one.

❷ 行って ください is the polite request form of 行く.

❸ です is the polite form of the copula.

❹ ね is a particle used when the speaker is confirming something.

4 次の 角を 右に 曲がって ください。…それから、あの ガソリンスタンドを 左に 行って ください。
Please turn right at the next corner. Then take a left at that gas station.

❶ を is a particle used here to indicate a location along which someone/something moves.
公園を 通って、うちへ 帰った。 I went home through the park.

❷ に is a particle used here to indicate direction and is interchangeable with the particle へ.

❸ 曲がって ください is the polite request form of 曲がる.

5 その おすしやさんの 前で 止めてください。
Please stop in front of that sushi shop.

❶ おすしやさん is a polite, yet familiar, way of saying すしや (sushi shop.)

❷ で is a particle which here indicates where the action of the verb occurs.

6 2850円です。——これで お願いします。
That will be ¥2,850, please. –Here you are.

❶ これで means "with this," and is often used when handing over money for which change is required.

❷ お願いします is a polite way of asking somebody to do something.

7 ありがとう ございます。150円の おつりです。
Thank you. Here's ¥150 change.

150円の おつり The particle の functions like "of" in this case, i.e. change of ¥150.

8 あ、お客さん、忘れものですよ。
Oh, ma'am, you forgot something.

❶ お客さん is the polite form of 客, used here to directly address a passenger.

❷ よ is a particle that gives emphasis to the sentence.

9 そうだ、雑誌を 忘れる ところだった。どうも すみません。——ありがとう ございました。
Oh! I was about to forget my magazine. Thank you. –Thank you.

❶ ところ means "place" but is often used fronted by a verb to describe a time or state.

Preceded by plain form verb and followed by だ／です:

i) 晩ごはんを 食べる ところだ／です。   I am just about to eat supper.

ii) 晩ごはんを 食べた ところだ／です。   I have just eaten supper.

Preceded by verb in ongoing action form and followed by だ／です:

i) 先生と 話して いる ところ だ／です。   I am talking with my teacher.

ii) 先生と 話して いた ところ だ／です。   I have just been talking with my teacher.

When preceded by a plain verb form only, and followed by the だった／でした past form of the copula, it normally indicates a state or time that almost came about.

終電車に 乗り遅れる ところだった／でした。   I almost missed the last train.

❷ すみません, which is often used to mean sorry, can also be used, as here, to thank people for their trouble.

DRILLS

1. 質問に 答えなさい。
   Answer the following questions.

1 だれが 終電車に 乗り遅れましたか。
   → (　　　　　　　) です。

2 スミスさんは 何を 利用して、うちへ 帰りましたか。
   → (　　　　　　　) を 利用して、うちへ 帰りました。

3 おつりは いくらでしたか。
   → (　　　　　　　) 円でした。

4 スミスさんは 何を 忘れる ところでしたか。
   → (　　　　　　　) を 忘れる ところでした。

2. 正しい 語を 選んで、次の 文章を 完成させなさい。
   Complete the following passage by selecting the most appropriate word.

今朝 早く 同級生の 和男君の うちへ 行った。和男君は ちょうど (**1** 起きて いる／起きた) ところで、まだ 眠そうだった。和男君と コーヒーを (**2** 飲んで いる／飲む) ところに インディラさんが やってきた。午後 三人で 東京ディズニーランドへ 行った。とても 楽しかった。夜 遅くまで 遊んだので、もう 少しで 終電車に (**3** 乗り遅れる／乗り遅れた) ところだった。

VOCABULARY

- だれ who
- が particle to indicate the subject of a sentence
- 乗(の)り遅(おく)れました missed [the train]
- 何(なに) what
- 帰(かえ)りました returned [home]
- いくら how much
- でした was, were
- 今朝(けさ) this morning
- 早(はや)く early
- 同級生(どうきゅうせい) classmate
- 和男(かずお) is a given name and 君(くん) is a masculine suffix used for boys
- 行(い)った went
- ちょうど just
- 起(お)きて いる is up
- 起(お)きた got up
- で being
- まだ still, yet
- 眠(ねむ)そう looking sleepy
- だった was, were
- と with
- コーヒー coffee
- 飲(の)んで いる is drinking
- 飲(の)む to drink
- に at [the time of]
- インディラ Indila
- やってきた came
- 午後(ごご) in the afternoon, P.M.
- 三人(さんにん)で with three [of us]: 人 is a counter for people
- 東京(とうきょう)ディズニーランド Tokyo Disneyland
- とても very [much]
- 楽(たの)しかった was enjoyable
- 夜(よる) [at] night
- 遅(おそ)く late
- まで until
- 遊(あそ)んだ played
- ので because
- もう 少(すこ)しで just by a little
- 乗(の)り遅(おく)れる to miss [the train]

TASKS

1. これ、それ、あれ、どれ？
   This one, that one, that one over there, which one?

☐ の 中の ことばを 使って、下の 会話を 完成させなさい。

Complete the dialogues by adding the words in the box below.

```
これ  この  ここ  それ  その  そこ  あれ  あの  あそこ
```

1 A：あのう、すみません。電話は どこに ありますか。
　 B：ああ、電話ですか。(**a**　　) に ありますよ。
　　 (**b**　　) 木の むこうに あります。

2 A：(**c**　　) は 何ですか。
　 B：バラです。(**d**　　) は プレゼントです。

3 A：きれいですね。
　　 (**e**　　) には たくさん 花が さいて いますね。
　 B：(**f**　　) 花は すみれですか。
　 A：いいえ、(**g**　　) は スイートピーですよ。

4 A：Bさん、あなたの 本は (**h**　　) ですか、
　　 (**i**　　) ですか。
　 B：(**j**　　) です。(**k**　　) 黒い カバーの 本です。
　　 Aさんの 本は あの 白い カバーの 本ですよ。

VOCABULARY

- 中 (なか) inside
- ことば word, language
- 使 (つか) って using
- 下 (した) below
- 完成 (かんせい) させなさい complete: an imperative form
- これ this one
- それ that one
- あれ that one over there
- この this __
- その that __
- あの that __ over there
- ここ here, this place
- そこ there, that place
- あそこ that place over there
- あのう、すみません say, excuse me
- 電話 (でんわ) telephone [call]
- どこ where
- に in, at, on
- あります there is, to exist
- ああ oh, ah
- 木 (き) tree
- むこう beyond
- バラ rose
- プレゼント present, gift
- きれい beautiful, pretty
- たくさん many, much
- 花 (はな) flower
- さいて います to be in bloom
- すみれ violet
- いいえ no
- スイートピー sweet pea
- あなた you
- 本 (ほん) book
- 黒 (くろ) い black
- カバー cover
- 白 (しろ) い white

2. 子供服売り場
Children's fashion department

　ここは ふじデパートの 三階 子供服売り場です。南側に エレベーターが 二台 あります。西の エレベーターから 出て、まっすぐ 行くと、つきあたりは 男の 子の スーツ売り場 です。その 手前で 男女の ズボンを 売って います。まん中に 男女の シャツの カウンターが あり、その 後ろが 女の 子の ブラウスの カウンターです。東の エレベーターを 出ると、左に アクセサリーや ハンカチ、右に パジャマの 売り場が あり、その 奥が スカートの カウンターです。ワンピースは 右奥に あります。男女の 下着は 西の エレベーターの 左側で、くつしたは その 右側です。
次の ものは どの カウンターで 売って いますか。

After reading the passage above, write in the number of the correct counter where each of the following items is sold.

a スーツ　　　　（　）
b ブラウス　　　（　）
c 下着　　　　　（　）
d ズボン　　　　（　）
e スカート　　　（　）
f パジャマ　　　（　）
g シャツ　　　　（　）
h ワンピース　　（　）
i くつした　　　（　）
j アクセサリー　（　）

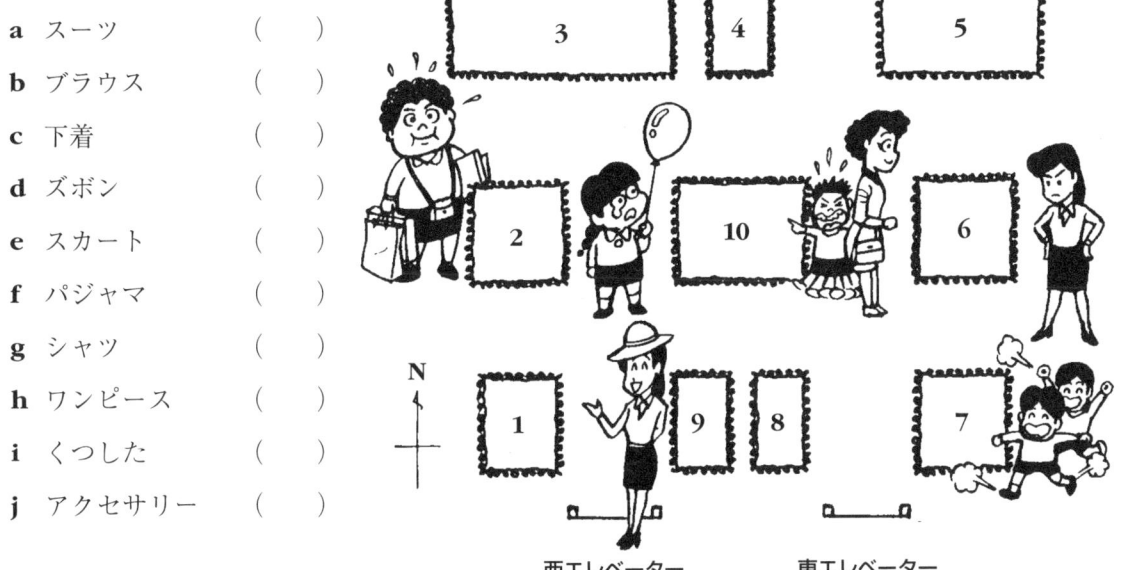

西エレベーター　　東エレベーター

VOCABULARY		
●ここ here, this place	●男(おとこ)の 子(こ) boy	●左(ひだり) left
●ふじデパート Fuji Department Store	●スーツ suit	●アクセサリー jewelry
●三階(さんがい) third floor	●手前(てまえ) before	●や and so on
●子供服(こどもふく) children's clothing	●男女(だんじょ) male and female	●ハンカチ handkerchief
●売(う)り場(ば) counter	●ズボン pants, trousers	●右(みぎ) right
●南側(みなみがわ) south side	●売(う)って います is selling	●パジャマ pajamas
●エレベーター elevator	●まん中(なか) the middle, the center	●奥(おく) the back
●二台(にだい) two [machines]: 台 is a counter for machinery	●シャツ shirt	●スカート skirt
	●カウンター counter	●ワンピース dress
●西(にし) west	●あり there being, existing	●下着(したぎ) underwear
●から from	●後(うし)ろ back, behind	●で being
●出(で)て going out, leaving	●女(おんな)の 子(こ) girl	●くつした socks
●まっすぐ straight	●ブラウス blouse	●次(つぎ) next, following
●行(い)くと if [you] go	●東(ひがし) east	●もの thing, object
●つきあたり the end	●出(で)る to go out, to leave	●どの which __

9 これ どうぞ — This is for you.

DIALOGUE

VOCABULARY

- 佐藤さん Mr. Sato
- は as for, speaking of
- 先週 last week
- スミスさん Ms. Smith
- に here, agent particle
- アメリカ America, the United States
- の of
- フルーツケーキ fruit cake
- もらった received
- その that
- お礼に in gratitude
- に to
- おもち rice cake
- あげる to give
- ことに した decided to
- ○ピンポーン sound of the door bell
- これ this [one]
- どうぞ please
- ずいぶん very
- 重い heavy
- です is, are, am
- ね isn't it?
- 何 what
- かしら I wonder
- 九州 Kyushu
- 母 [my] mother
- 送って くれた sent

OBJECTIVES:
Introducing verbs of giving and receiving.

- そうですか Really? Is that so?
- ありがとう ございます Thank you
- わたし I
- も also
- ご両親 [your, someone's] parents
- 何か something
- さしあげたい to want to give
- が [weak] but
- いい good
- どうぞ ご心配なく Don't worry
- おいしい delicious
- いただいた received
- ところです just [did ~]
- から because, so
- あの that _
- 半分 half
- 両親へ to [my] parents
- 送って やった sent
- よ you know
- とても very
- 喜んで いました was glad
- じゃ then
- もっと more
- もらいます to receive
- ホホッ、ハハハ sound of laughter

CULTURE

Gift-giving

Gift-giving in Japan is considered a mainly reciprocal way of reinforcing relationships with friends, neighbors, and colleagues. As well as during specific gift-giving seasons such as midsummer *o-chuugen* and end-of-year *o-seibo*, suitable gifts are also offered whenever favor, patronage, or support is sought. New neighbors, for example, may give presents to nearby residents, students may think it wise to offer gifts to their teachers, and shopkeepers may see the business sense in rewarding regular customers for their loyalty. Until recently, *o-chuugen* and *o-seibo* gifts were typically expensive, "brand-name" toiletries, tableware, and foreign liquor, but since recession tightened purse strings, many now prefer to give and receive boxed sets of beer, salad oil, and even soap detergents. Whatever the occasion, it is often the case that all gifts are eventually returned with items of similar value.

PRONUNCIATION

Listen to the tape and repeat. High pitches are marked with ⌈ and low pitches with ⌉. All words appearing in **bold** should be stressed. Note that hyphenated phrases are treated as one word.

1 Satoo-san-wa senshuu Sumisu-san-ni Amerika-no **furuutsu-keeki**-o moratta.

Sono oree-ni Satoo-san-wa Sumisu-san-ni **o-mochi**-o ageru koto-ni shita.

2 Sumisu-san, **kore** doozo.

3 Zuibun omoi-desu-ne. Nani-kashira.

4 O-mochi-desu. Kyuushuu-no **haha**-ga okutte kureta-n-desu.

5 Soo-desu-ka. **Arigatoo** gozaimasu.

Watashi-mo Satoo-san-no go-ryooshin-ni nanika sashiage-tai-n-desu-ga, **nani**-ga ii-kashira.

6 **Doozo** go-shinpai-naku. Senshuu oishii Amerika-no **furuutsu-keeki**-o itadaita tokoro-desu-kara.

7 Ano keeki-wa **hanbun** ryooshin-e okutte yatta-n-desu-yo. Ryooshin-mo totemo **yorokonde** imashita.

8 Soo-desu-ka. Ja, Amerika-no ryooshin-ni **motto** okutte moraimasu.

NOTES

1 佐藤さんは 先週 スミスさんに アメリカの フルーツケーキを もらった。
その お礼に 佐藤さんは スミスさんに おもちを あげる ことに した。
Mr. Sato received an American fruit cake from Ms. Smith last week.
In gratitude, Mr. Sato decided to give Ms. Smith rice cakes.

❶ を is the direct object particle, indicating the person or thing to whom the action of the verb is done.

❷ もらった is the plain past form of もらう. あげる means "to give." (See below.)

Giving and receiving verbs:

There are two types of so-called giving verbs: (i) やる・あげる・さしあげる　(ii) くれる・くださる

やる— Someone gives to an inferior.
　わたしは 弟に 映画の チケットを やった。 I gave a movie ticket to my younger brother.
あげる— Someone gives to an equal.
　その お礼に 佐藤さんは スミスさんに おもちを あげる ことに した。 (See above.)
さしあげる— Someone gives to a superior.
　わたしも 佐藤さんの ご両親に 何か さしあげたいんですが、何が いいかしら。 (See **5**.)
くれる— An equal or inferior gives to the speaker or the speaker's "in-group" members.
　弟は わたしに 映画の チケットを くれた。 My younger brother gave me a ticket for a film.
くださる— A superior gives to the speaker or the speaker's "in-group" members.
　鈴木先生が 姉に 本を くださった。 Professor Suzuki gave a book to my older sister.

The receiving verbs are もらう and いただく.

もらう— Someone receives something from an inferior or equal.
　佐藤さんは 先週 スミスさんに／(から) アメリカの フルーツケーキを もらった。 (See above.)
いただく— Someone receives something from a superior.
　先週 おいしい アメリカの フルーツケーキを いただいた ところですから。 (See **6**.)

The person from whom someone receives is marked by one of two particles に or から.

Giving and receiving verbs often follow the て-／で-form of verbs when the verb's action is perceived as a favor either given or received. (See **4** **7** and **8** as examples.)

❸ ことに した is the plain past form of ことに する.

2 スミスさん、これ どうぞ。
Ms. Smith, this is for you.

これ どうぞ is missing the direct object particle を, since spoken Japanese often does away with it.

3 ずいぶん 重いですね。何かしら。
It's quite heavy. I wonder what it is.

❶ 重い is an い-adjective.
❷ です is the polite form of the copula.
❸ ね is a particle used by the speaker to confirm something.
❹ (何)かしら is normally used by women, while men use (何)かな.

4 おもちです。九州の 母が 送って くれたんです。
They're rice cakes. My mother who lives in Kyushu sent them.

- ❶ が is a particle that marks the subject.
- ❷ 送って is the て-form of the verb 送る.
- ❸ くれた is the plain past tense of くれる.
- ❹ んです gives the sentence an explanatory and emphatic feel. (See **2**-❸ in Notes to Module 4.)

5 そうですか。ありがとう ございます。
わたしも 佐藤さんの ご両親に 何か さしあげたいんですが、何が いいかしら。
Really. Thank you. I would also like to give something to your parents. What do you think would be good?

- ❶ も is a particle meaning "also."
- ❷ ご両親 is the honorific form of 両親. (See Notes to Module 7.)
- ❸ さしあげたい is the たい-form of the giving verb さしあげる. (See Notes to Module 4 for the たい-form of wanting to do something.)
- ❹ (んです)が が (weak "but") here is a conjunction often used with the たい-form to soften the assertion.
- ❺ いい is an い-adjective.

6 どうぞ ご心配なく。先週 おいしい アメリカの フルーツケーキを いただいたところ ですから。
You don't need to bother. You just gave me a delicious American fruit cake last week.

- ❶ おいしい is an い-adjective.
- ❷ いただいた is the plain past form of いただく.
- ❸ ところです is used to describe a time or state. (See Notes to Module 8.)
- ❹ から here is a conjunction meaning "because."

7 あの ケーキは 半分 両親へ 送って やったんですよ。両親も とても 喜んで いました。
I sent half of it to my parents. They were very pleased.

- ❶ あの here refers to something both speaker and listener are aware of.
- ❷ へ is a particle here that indicates direction: In this case it clarifies to whom some cake was sent.
- ❸ やった is the plain past form of やる.
- ❹ よ is a particle used here to add emphasis.
- ❺ 喜んで いました is the polite past form of 喜んで いる, the -て いる form of 喜ぶ (See Notes in Vocabulary on p.56.)

8 そうですか。じゃ、アメリカの 両親に もっと 送って もらいます。
Is that so? I will have my parents send more from the United States!

もらいます is the polite form of もらう.

DRILLS

1. 質問に 答えなさい。
Answer the following questions.

1 だれが スミスさんに アメリカの フルーツケーキを もらいましたか。 → （　　）です。

2 佐藤さんは スミスさんに 何を あげる ことに しましたか。 → （　　）です。

3 スミスさんは アメリカの ご両親に 何を もっと 送って もらいますか。 → （　　）です。

2. 次の 絵を 見て、正しい 語を 選んで 入れなさい。
Using the picture, fill in the blanks with the most appropriate word.

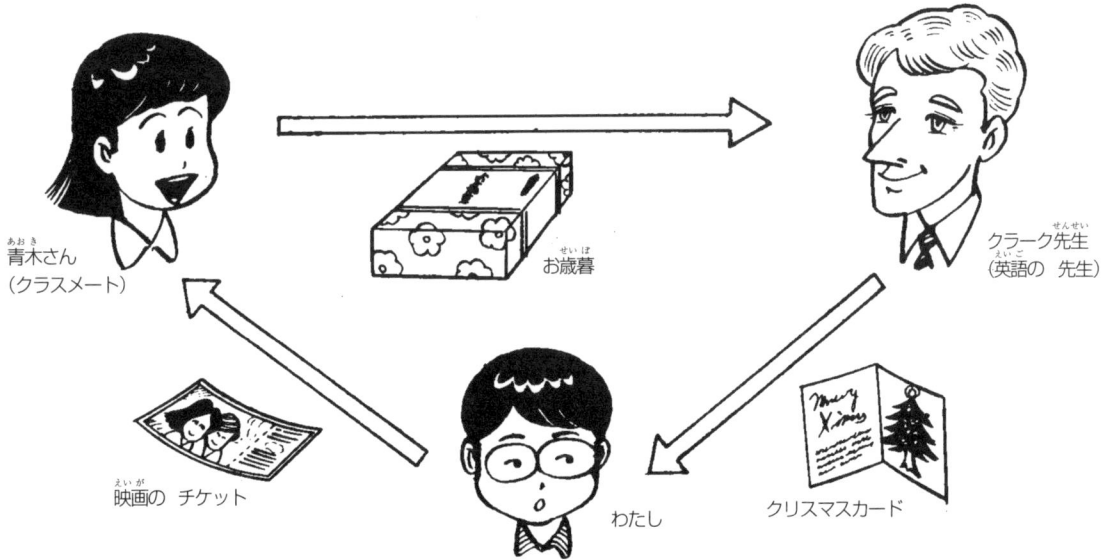

| くださいました　あげました　いただきました　さしあげました　もらいました |

1 わたしは 青木さんに 映画の チケットを （　　　　　）。

2 青木さんは クラーク先生に お歳暮を （　　　　　）。

3 クラーク先生は わたしに クリスマスカードを （　　　　　）。

4 クラーク先生は 青木さんに／から お歳暮を （　　　　　）。

5 わたしは クラーク先生に／から クリスマスカードを （　　　　　）。

VOCABULARY
- だれ　who
- もらいました　received
- 何(なに)　what
- ことに しました　decided to
- お歳暮(せいぼ)　year-end gift
- 青木(あおき)さん　Ms. Aoki
- クラスメート　classmate
- クラーク先生(せんせい)　Professor Clark
- 英語(えいご)　English
- 映画(えいが)　movie
- チケット　ticket
- クリスマスカード　Christmas card
- から　from
- くださいました　gave
- あげました　gave
- いただきました　received
- さしあげました　gave

T A S K S

1. ゆき子さんと マイクさん
Yukiko and Mike

次の まんがを よく 見て、正しい 語を 選びなさい。

Using the comic-strip as a guide, select the most appropriate words from the alternatives in parentheses.

1 今年の 夏 ゆき子さんは 海で マイクさんに 助けて（もらった・あげた）ので、
マイクさんに プレゼントを（もらいました・あげました）。

2 マイクさんは ゆき子さんに「日本語を 教えて（あげませんか・くれませんか）。」と
言いました。
ゆき子さんは マイクさんから 英語を 教えて（あげました・もらいました）。

3 マイクさんの 誕生日に ゆき子さんは お母さんに 教えて（もらって・くれて）、
フルーツケーキを 作って（もらいました・あげました）。セーターも 編んで
（もらいました・あげました）。

4 マイクさんは ゆき子さんに「ぼくと 結婚して（くれませんか・あげませんか）。」と
言いました。二人は 来年 結婚する 予定です。

VOCABULARY

- 次（つぎ） next, following
- まんが comics
- よく well
- 見（み）て looking at
- 正（ただ）しい correct
- 語（ご） word
- 選（えら）びなさい
  choose: an imperative form
- 今年（ことし） this year
- 夏（なつ） summer
- 海（うみ） ocean, sea
- で in, at, on

- 助（たす）けて saving
- もらった received
- あげた gave
- 〜ので because 〜
- プレゼント present, gift
- 日本語（にほんご） Japanese language
- 教（おし）えて teaching
- あげませんか／くれませんか
  would you give a favor of 〜
- 言（い）いました said
- 誕生日（たんじょうび）に
  on [one's] birthday

- もらって receiving
- くれて giving
- 作（つく）って making
- セーター sweater
- 編（あ）んで knitting
- ぼく [masculine] I
- 〜と 結婚（けっこん）して
  getting married to 〜
- 二人（ふたり） two persons
- 来年（らいねん） next year
- 予定（よてい） plan

2. お歳暮
Year-end gifts

田中さんと 小川さんが 護国寺デパートの 1990年から 1994年までの お歳暮(1位〜3位)の 変化に ついて 話を して います。話を よく 読んで、正しい グラフを 選びなさい。

Mr. Tanaka and Ms. Ogawa are discussing changes in the sales ranking of year-end gifts sold at Gokokuji Department Store between 1990 and 1994. Read their conversation and select the correct graph.

田中：5年前は 商品券より おかしを あげる 人が 多かったんだね。ぼくは おかしより ビールを もらった ほうが うれしいな。毎年 ビールを あげる 人が 一番 多いと 思ったけど。

小川：いいえ、最近は 商品券を あげる 人が 増えて いるのよ。ほら、去年は ビールより 商品券の ほうが 多いわ。わたしも 今年の お歳暮 商品券を もらいたいわ。ね、田中さん！

田中：えっ！？

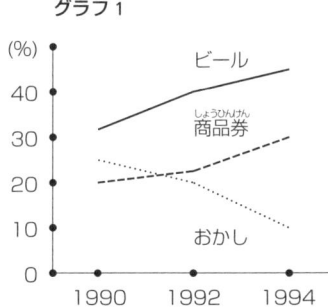
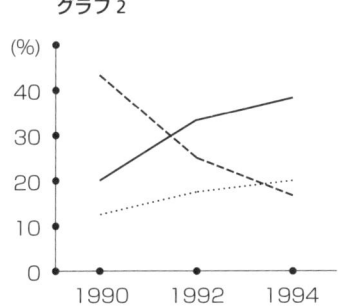
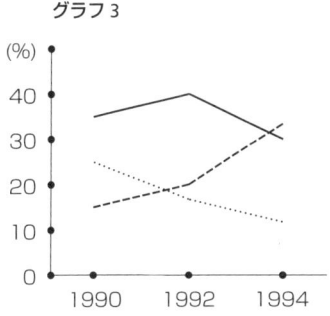

VOCABULARY

- 田中(たなか) and 小川(おがわ) are both family names.
- と and
- 護国寺(ごこくじ)デパート Gokokuji Department Store
- 1990年(ねん) the year of 1990
- 去年(きょねん) last year
- まで until
- 1位(いちい)、3位(さんい) are the first place and the third place respectively
- 変化(へんか) change
- 〜に ついて about 〜
- 話(はなし) talk, story
- して います is doing
- よく well
- 読(よ)んで reading
- グラフ graph
- 5年前(ごねんまえ) five years ago
- 商品券(しょうひんけん) gift certificate
- より [more] than
- おかし sweets
- 人(ひと) person
- 多(おお)かった were many
- んだ you know
- ビール beer
- ほう alternative
- うれしい glad, happy
- な you know, I should say
- 毎年(まいとし) every year
- 一番(いちばん) most, to the greatest degree, no. 1
- 〜と that 〜
- 思(おも)った thought
- けど [weak] but
- いいえ no
- 最近(さいきん) recently
- 増(ふ)えて いる is increasing
- 〜のよ you know
- ほら Look!
- わ particle used by a female speaker to express her weak assertion or volition
- もらいたい to want to receive
- えっ What? Oh!

10 今年も どうぞ よろしく

I look forward to our continued relationship over this year.

DIALOGUE

1. キムさんは 郵便局で ぐうぜん 鈴木先生に 会った。鈴木先生は 孫の 愛子ちゃんと いっしょだった。

2. あ、鈴木先生、明けまして おめでとう ございます。
   やあ、キムさん、おめでとう。

3. 今年も どうぞ よろしく お願い いたします。
   こちらこそ どうぞ よろしく。

4. 孫が いろんな 方に たくさん お年玉を いただいたので、預けに 来た ところです。
   孫の 愛子です。

VOCABULARY

- キムさん Ms. Kim
- は as for, speaking of
- 郵便局 past office
- で at, in, on
- ぐうぜん accidentally, by chance
- 鈴木先生 Professor Suzuki
- 〜に 会った met 〜
- 孫 grandchild
- の of
- 愛子ちゃん Aiko
- 〜と いっしょ together with 〜
- だった was, were
- ガーッ sound of automatic door
- あ Oh! Ah!
- 明けまして おめでとう ございます Happy New Year!
- やあ oh, hello
- 今年も どうぞ よろしく お願い いたします I look forward to our continued relationship over this year
- こちらこそ it is I that
- いろんな various
- 方 person, people
- に by, from
- たくさん many, much
- お年玉 New Year's present [of money]
- いただいた received
- ので so, because
- 預けに for depositing
- 来た came

OBJECTIVES:
Introduction of conjunctions used in causal relationships and using the particle に to express purpose.

- ところ just [did]
- です is, are, am
- ○ニッ sound-effect word for smiling face
- わたし I
- 元旦 New Year's Day
- に on, at, in
- 明治神宮 the Meiji Shrine
- 撮った took [a photo]
- 写真 photo
- 国 [one's] country
- へ to
- 送ろう to intend to send
- 〜と 思って thinking that 〜
- 来ました came
- そうですか Is that right?
- そうそう Oh, yes. I remember...
- 今度 next [time]
- 土曜日 Saturday
- 午後 afternoon, P.M.
- から from
- うち [my] house, home
- 新年会 New Year's party
- する to do, to hold [a party]
- から because
- 来ませんか Would you like to come?
- はい yes
- ありがとう ございます Thank you
- ぜひ by all means
- うかがいます to visit

CULTURE

O-shoogatsu

At New Year or *o-shoogatsu*, all major highways, railroads, and airports are heavily congested as millions of Japanese leave major cities and head back to their hometowns in order to fortify family ties, honor their ancestors, and pray at the local shrine for good luck in the coming year. Many Japanese will visit a Shinto shrine soon after midnight on New Year's Eve. *Hatsumoode*, the first visit to a shrine of the year, is an opportunity for people to dress up, ladies in traditional kimonos and gentlemen in smart, new suits. Children look forward to receiving *o-toshidama*, a cash gift wrapped in a special envelope, at this time of year, while adults are busy doing *nenshimawari*, formal calls on important and influential acquaintances like company superiors or local politicians. All enjoy the special New Year's food known as *o-sechi ryoori* that is prepared a few days before *o-shoogatsu* and served in decorated boxes.

PRONUNCIATION

Listen to the tape and repeat. High pitches are marked with ⌐ and low pitches with ⌐. All words appearing in **bold** should be stressed. Note that hyphenated phrases are treated as one word.

1. Kimu-san-wa yuubinkyoku-de guuzen **Suzuki-sensee**-ni atta.

    Suzuki-sensee-wa mago-no **Aiko-chan**-to issho-datta.

2. A, Suzuki-sensee, akemashite **omedetoo** gozaimasu.

    Yaa, Kimu-san, **omedetoo**.

3. Kotoshi-mo doozo **yoroshiku** onegai-itashimasu.

    Kochira-koso doozo **yoroshiku**.

4. Mago-ga ironna kata-ni takusan otoshidama-o itadaita-node, **azuke**-ni kita tokoro-desu.

    Mago-no **Aiko**-desu.

5. Akemashite **omedetoo** gozaimasu.

    Omedetoo, Aiko-chan.

6. Watashi-wa gantan-ni Meeji-jinguu-de totta shashin-o **kuni**-e okuroo-to omotte kimashita.

7. Soo-desu-ka. Soosoo, kondo-no doyoobi-ni gogo-kara uchi-de **shinnen-kai**-o suru-kara, kimasen-ka.

8. Hai, **arigatoo** gozaimasu. Zehi, **ukagaimasu**.

NOTES

1 キムさんは 郵便局で ぐうぜん 鈴木先生に 会った。鈴木先生は 孫の 愛子ちゃんと いっしょだった。
Ms. Kim bumped into Prof. Suzuki at the post office. Prof. Suzuki was with his granddaughter, Aiko.

❶ は is a particle marking the topic of the sentence. (See Notes to Module 1.)
❷ Here, the particle で indicates where the action of the verb takes place.
❸ に 会った is the plain past form of (somebody) に 会う.
❹ の is a particle that, here, marks the noun that modifies or describes the noun that follows の.
❺ -ちゃん is a suffix usually added to children's names, but also pets and female friends, to indicate affection and familiarity.
❻ だった is the plain past form of copula.

2 あ、鈴木先生、明けまして おめでとう ございます。──やあ、キムさん、おめでとう。
Oh, Professor Suzuki! Happy New Year! – Hello, Ms. Kim. Happy New Year!

おめでとう ございます is the general way of expressing congratulations, and can be shortened to おめでとう in less formal situations, in particular addressing to an inferior.

3 今年も どうぞ よろしく お願いいたします。──こちらこそ どうぞ よろしく。
I look forward to our continued relationship over this year. –I do, too.

どうぞ よろしく お願いいたします is a common phrase used when meeting somebody for the first time or seeking new or continued support from somebody.

4 孫が いろんな 方に たくさん お年玉を いただいたので、預けに 来た ところです。孫の 愛子です。
My granddaughter received many gifts of money for New Year's and we have come to deposit them. This is my granddaughter, Aiko.

❶ が is a particle that introduces the subject.
❷ いろんな is a な-adjective.
❸ 方 is the honorific term for 人 (person).
❹ に is a particle that when used with いただく or もらう, as here, indicates from whom someone received something. (See Notes in Module 9.)
❺ を is a particle that marks the direct object.
❻ いただいた is the plain past form of いただく.
❼ ので, in this case, is a conjunction corresponding to "because."

ので and から are used to connect sentences that have a causal relationship. Of the two, ので sounds more polite and formal, as it has a more objective quality than から. から normally precedes sentences expressing strong desire or suggestion on the speaker's part.

ので─きのう おすしを 食べたので、今日は 食べません。 I ate sushi yesterday, so I won't eat it today.
から─高く ありませんから、もう 一つ 買いましょう。 They are not expensive, so let's buy one more.

Note that though から can be used with sentences ending in からだ/からです to emphasize the reason/cause, ので can not.

Thus: 電車に 乗り遅れたので／から タクシーで 帰りました。
I went home by taxi because I missed the train.

Becomes: タクシーで 帰ったのは、電車に 乗り遅れたからです。
The reason why I went home by taxi was because I had missed the train.

You cannot say: 乗り遅れたのでです.

❽ 飲けに When に is attached to the bound form of the verb, it shows purpose.
日曜日に 友だちと ビールを 飲みに 行った。 I went to drink beer with my friend on Sunday.

❾ 来た is the plain past form of 来る.

❿ ところ is used to describe a time or state. (See Notes in Module 8.)

⓫ です is the polite form of the copula.

5 明けまして おめでとう ございます。——おめでとう、愛子ちゃん。
Happy New Year! –Happy New Year, Aiko.

明けまして comes from 年が 明ける, meaning "a new year is beginning or dawning."

6 わたしは 元旦に 明治神宮で 撮った 写真を 国へ 送ろうと 思って 来ました。
I came [to the post office] to send home some photos that I took at the Meiji Shrine on New Year's Day.

❶ に is a particle that here marks the time or occasion when the action of the verb took place.

❷ 送ろう is the [y]oo form of 送る. (See Notes to Module 4.)

❸ と is a particle used to quote the direct or indirect words, thoughts, and ideas of the speaker.

❹ 思って is the て-form of 思う, used here to connect the clauses and indicates a reason for the action of the verb.

❺ 来ました is the polite past form of the verb 来る.

7 そうですか。そうそう、今度の 土曜日に 午後から うちで 新年会を するから、来ませんか。
Oh, really? Oh, I just remembered we're having a New Year's party at my home this Saturday afternoon. Would you like to come?

❶ から is a particle here indicating the time from when the action of the verb will take place.

❷ The second から in the sentence is a conjunction indicating reason or cause. (See Notes to **4**.)

❸ 来ません is the polite negative form of 来る.

❹ か, when attached to a polite negative form such as 来ません, indicates the speaker is inviting the listener to do something.

8 はい、ありがとう ございます。ぜひ うかがいます。
Thank you. I would love to come.

うかがいます is the polite form of うかがう, meaning "to come or go" when the speaker is humbly referring to himself.

DRILLS

1. 質問に 答えなさい。
Answer the following questions.

1 キムさんは 郵便局で だれに 会いましたか。
 → (　　　　　　) に 会いました。

2 鈴木先生は だれと いっしょでしたか。
 → (　　　　　　) と いっしょでした。

3 キムさんは 国へ 何を 送ろうと 思って いますか。
 → (　　　　　　) を 送ろうと 思って います。

4 だれの うちで 新年会を しますか。
 → (　　　　　　) の うちです。

2. 「ので」または「から」を 使って、次の 会話を 完成させなさい。
Using either ので or から, complete the following dialogue.

A 初詣は どこかへ 行きましたか。

B ええ、着物を 着て、近くの お寺へ 行きました。でも、雪が 降って いた (**a**　　　)、たいへんでした。

A そうですか。ところで、今度の 日曜日に うちで 新年会を します (**b**　　　)、ぜひ 来て ください。

B ありがとう ございます。でも、行けないかもしれません。

A どうしてですか。

B 学校の 宿題が たくさん たまって いる (**c**　　　) です。

VOCABULARY

- だれ who
- 会(あ)いました met
- でした was, were
- 何(なに、なん) what
- 思(おも)って います is thinking
- します to do, to hold
- 初詣(はつもうで) the first visit to a shrine (temple) during the New Year holidays
- どこか somewhere
- 行(い)きました went
- ええ yes
- 着物(きもの) kimono
- 着(き)て wearing
- 近(ちか)く nearby
- お寺(てら) temple
- でも but, however
- 雪(ゆき) snow
- 降(ふ)って いた was falling
- たいへん hard, troublesome
- ところで by the way
- 日曜日(にちようび) Sunday
- します to do, to hold
- 来(き)て ください please come
- 行(い)けない cannot go
- 〜かもしれません might
- どうして why
- 学校(がっこう) school
- 宿題(しゅくだい) homework, assignment
- たまって いる is piled up

TASKS

1. 何を しに 行ったか。
What did you go and do?

次の 表現を 使って、下の 文を 完成させなさい。

Using the phrases **a** to **l** below, complete the following sentences.

a 探しに 行った	**b** 出しに 行った	**c** たのみに 行った
d 飲みに 行った	**e** しに 行った	**f** 見に 行った
g 助けに 行った	**h** 預けに 行った	**i** 食べに 行った
j 撮りに 行った	**k** 書きに 行った	**l** 作りに 行った

1　お年玉を たくさん もらったので、銀行へ_____。

2　猫が いなく なったので、_____。

3　土曜日に 友だちと 映画を _____。

4　手紙を 書いて、郵便局へ _____。

5　中田さんと バーへ_____。

6　太郎と グラウンドへ キャッチボールを _____。

7　犬が 川へ 落ちたので、_____。

8　公園へ 写真を _____。

VOCABULARY

- ●次(つぎ) next, following
- ●表現(ひょうげん) phrase, expression
- ●使(つか)って using
- ●下(した) below
- ●文(ぶん) sentence
- ●完成(かんせい)させなさい complete: an imperative form
- ●探(さが)し looking for
- ●出(だ)し mailing, sending
- ●たのみ asking
- ●飲(の)み drinking
- ●見(み) watching, seeing
- ●助(たす)け saving, helping
- ●食(た)べ eating
- ●撮(と)り taking [a photo]
- ●書(か)き writing
- ●作(つく)り making
- ●もらった received
- ●銀行(ぎんこう) bank
- ●猫(ねこ) cat
- ●いなく なった disappeared
- ●友(とも)だち friend[s]
- ●と [together] with
- ●映画(えいが) movie
- ●手紙(てがみ) letter
- ●書(か)いて writing
- ●中田(なかだ)さん Mr./Ms. Nakada
- ●バー bar
- ●太郎(たろう) Taro
- ●グラウンド ground, field
- ●キャッチボール catch
- ●犬(いぬ) dog
- ●川(かわ) river
- ●落(お)ちた fell
- ●公園(こうえん) park

2. だれと だれが いつ どこで 会ったか。
Who met whom when and where?

インディラと エドワードと あきらの 日記を 読んで、だれが だれと 何時ごろ どこで 会ったか 下の 表に 書き入れなさい。

Read the three diary entries below and then supply the missing information in the chart at the bottom of the page.

[インディラの 日記]
ゴルフ場へ 朝 9時に 行った。午後 1時に ゴルフ場の レストランで お昼ごはんを 食べた。それから、田中さんと 4時まで テニスを した。二人で カラオケへ 行って、8時 15分ごろ レストラン・サンで 晩ごはんを 食べた。

[エドワードの 日記]
7時に ゴルフに 行った。12時に ゴルフ場の レストランで ごはんを 食べて、1時に 帰った。2時半から キャシーと テニスを して、6時に レストラン・サンで 夕食。8時に 帰って、二人で 音楽を 聞いた。

[あきらの 日記]
8時から 10時まで そうじと せんたく。12時 30分まで ジョギング。3時から 弟と ドライブに 行き、6時 15分に レストラン・サンで 夕食。8時ごろ うちへ 帰った。

	だれと だれが	何時から 何時ごろ	どこで	会った
1		9時から 12時ごろ	2	会った
3		4	テニスコートで	会った
5		6	レストラン・サンで	会った

VOCABULARY

- インディラ (Indila), エドワード (Edward), あきら are all first names.
- 日記 (にっき) diary
- 読 (よ) んで reading
- だれ who
- 何時 (なんじ) ごろ about what time
- 下 (した) below
- 表 (ひょう) chart
- 書 (か) き入 (い) れなさい write/fill in: an imperative form
- ゴルフ場 (じょう) golf course
- 朝 (あさ) [in the] morning
- ～時 (じ) に at ～ o'clock
- 午後 (ごご) [in the] afternoon, P.M.
- レストラン restaurant
- お昼 (ひる) ごはん lunch
- 食 (た) べた ate
- それから and then, after that
- 田中 (たなか) さん Ms. Tanaka
- まで until
- テニス tennis
- 二人 (ふたり) で by two persons
- カラオケ karaoke music place
- 分 (ふん、ぷん) minute[s]
- レストラン・サン Restaurant Sun
- 晩 (ばん) ごはん supper, dinner
- 食 (た) べて eating
- 帰 (かえ) った returned [home]
- 半 (はん) half
- キャシー Cathy
- して doing, playing
- 夕食 (ゆうしょく) supper
- 音楽 (おんがく) music
- 聞 (き) いた listened
- ～から～まで from~until~
- そうじ cleaning
- せんたく washing
- ジョギング jogging
- 弟 (おとうと) [my] younger brother
- ドライブ drive
- 行 (い) き going
- うち home

11 お世話に なります

Thank you in advance.

DIALOGUE

1. 林さんは今朝見たアパートを借りたいが、決める前にもう一度見たいと思った。そこで、不動産屋の事務所へまたやってきた。

2. 今朝見せていただいたアパートなんですが…

3. はい、家賃も敷金も礼金もお話しした通りです。

4. あとは電気代とガス代と水道代ですね。

5. そうです。いいところでしょう。

ええ。

もじもじしている。

VOCABULARY

- 林さん Mr. Lin
- は as for, speaking of
- 今朝(けさ) this morning
- 見た saw
- アパート apartment [house]
- 借りたい to want to borrow
- 決める to decide
- 前に before
- もう一度 one more time, again
- 見たい to want to see
- と 思った thought that ~
- そこで then
- 不動産屋の 事務所 office of real estate agent
- へ to
- また again
- やってきた came along, came over
- ガラッ sound of the sliding door
- 見せて showing
- いただいた received [a favor]
- はい yes
- 家賃 rent
- も also
- 敷金 deposit
- 礼金 gift money, honorarium
- お話(はな)しした talked, told
- 通り as

OBJECTIVES:
Introducing humble forms, understanding the causative form and saying thank you.

- です is, are, am
- あと the rest
- 電気代 electric bill
- と and
- ガス gas
- 水道 water supply
- ね isn't it?
- そうです That's right
- いい good
- ところ place
- でしょう isn't it? will probably be
- ええ yes
- もじもじして いる is fidgeting
- どうでしょう How about...?
- 係 [the person] in charge
- 者 person
- 案内させましょうか
  Shall I have [him] take you over?
- お願いできます can do/ask a favor
- おい [masculine] Hey
- 山下君 Yamashita
- たのむ to ask [a favor]
- よ you know
- すみません
  Thank you [for your trouble], I'm sorry
- お世話に なります
  Thank you in advance

CULTURE

Renting apartments

As a first step to finding a home to rent in Japan, visit a real estate agent. Almost always located within five-minute walking distance of a railroad or subway station, the real estate office generally displays a selection of advertisements and room layouts of houses, apartments, and "manshon" condominiums in their store window. Before moving into an unfurnished and often unheated apartment, tenants must first pay the landlord "gift money", usually equivalent to two months' rent, a returnable deposit, typically also two months' rent, and finally the first month's rent in advance. The real estate agent will also charge a sum equal, in most cases, to one month's rent as his handling fee for arranging the letting of the apartment. All tenants must also sign a tenancy agreement with their landlord. This contract usually lasts for two years, but can often be extended indefinitely at two-year intervals.

PRONUNCIATION

Listen to the tape and repeat. High pitches are marked with ⌈ and low pitches with ⌉. All words appearing in **bold** should be stressed. Note that hyphenated phrases are treated as one word.

1 Rin-san-wa kesa mita apaato o kari-tai-ga, kimeru mae-ni **moo ichi-do** mi-tai-to omotta.

Sokode, **fudoosan-ya**-no jimusho-e mata yattekita.

2 **Kesa** misete itadaita apaato-nan-desu-ga...

3 Hai, yachin-mo shikikin-mo reekin-mo **ohanashi-shita** toori-desu.

4 Ato-wa **denki-dai**-to **gasu-dai**-to **suidoo-dai**-desu-ne.

5 Soo-desu. **Ii** tokoro-deshoo.

Ee.

6 Doo-deshoo. Moo ichi-do kakari-no mono-ni **annai**-sase-mashoo-ka.

7 **Onegai**-dekimasu-ka.

Ii-desu-yo. Oi, **Yamashita-kun**, tanomu-yo.

8 Sumimasen. **Osewa**-ni narimasu.

NOTES

1 林さんは 今朝 見た アパートを 借りたいが、決める 前に もう一度 見たいと 思った。そこで、不動産屋の 事務所へ また やってきた。
Mr. Lin wants to rent the apartment he saw this morning, but wants to look at it once more before making a decision. So he came to the real estate office again.

❶ は is a particle that here introduces the topic of the sentence. (See Notes to Module 1.)
❷ 見た is the plain past form of 見る.
❸ を is a particle indicating the direct object.
❹ 借りたい is the -たい form of 借りる. (See **2**-❷ in Notes to Module 4.)
❺ が is a conjunction here that is used like a weak "but." (See **3**-❸ in Notes to Module 6.)
❻ に is a particle used here to mark the time or occasion when the action of the verb takes place.
❼ 見たい is the -たい form of 見る.
❽ と is a particle used here to quote the speaker's words or unspoken thoughts and ideas.
❾ 思った is the plain past form of the verb 思う.
❿ の is a particle that marks the noun modifying or describing the noun after it.
⓫ へ is a particle that here shows physical direction.
⓬ やってきた is the plain past form of the verb やってくる.

2 今朝 見せて いただいた アパートなんですが…
About the apartment you showed me this morning...

❶ 見せて is the て-form of the verb 見せる.
❷ いただいた is the plain past form of いただく. (See Notes in Module 9)
❸ なんです attached to a noun or な-adjective provides emphasis and explanation with a colloquial flavor. (See Notes to Module 4.)
❹ が is used here as a conjunction to indicate an unsaid request or wish. (See **6**-❷ in Notes to Module 6.)

3 はい、家賃も 敷金も 礼金も お話しした 通りです。
Yes, the rent, deposit, and gift money are as I told you.

❶ も is a particle used here to mean "and" or "also."
❷ お話しした is the form of 話す used when the speaker wishes to sound humble. It is formed by sandwiching the bound form of the verb (i.e. with the -ます ending dropped) between the prefix お and the verb する.
❸ 通り indicates that the preceding information is correct or unchanged.
❹ です is the polite form of the copula.

4 あとは 電気代と ガス代と 水道代ですね。
And the rest are the fees for electricity, gas, and water, right?

❶ 代 attached to a noun means the fee or charge for it.
❷ と is a particle that here joins nouns like "and."
❸ ね is a particle used here by the speaker to confirm something.

5 そうです。いい ところでしょう。—ええ。(もじもじして いる。)
That's right. It's a nice place, isn't it? –Yes (fidgets.)

❶ いい is an い-adjective.

❷ でしょう here indicates that the speaker is seeking confirmation to his or her statement from the listener. However, whereas the particle ね is used mainly for confirmation of facts or circumstances, でしょう is used when the speaker is looking for (and often expecting) the listener to support an opinion.

❸ ええ is an informal version of はい.

❹ もじもじして いる is the て いる form of the ongoing action. (See Notes in Vocabulary on p.56.)

6 どうでしょう。もう 一度 係の 者に 案内させましょうか。
What do you think? Shall I have the person in charge take you over to see it again?

❶ に is a particle that marks the person who will perform the action of the verb.

❷ 案内させましょうか This is the suggestive form of 案内させる. The bound form of a verb+ましょうか— shall I/we do (something)?

案内させる is the so-called causative form of 案内する, and means to make/have/let somebody show something or give guidance.

The causative is formed by adding -(s)ase-ru/ -(s)ase-masu to the verb stem. As explained above, it can express the two very different ideas of getting somebody to do something or letting them do it. With intransitive verbs, the distinction is normally made by using を to indicate the person made to do something and に to mark the person allowed to do something.

わたしは 子どもを 買い物に 行かせます。　I'll make my child go shopping.
わたしは 子どもに 買い物に 行かせます。　I'll let my child go shopping.

However, such a distinction cannot be made with を in a transitive sentence.

わたしは 子どもに さしみを 食べさせた。　I made/let my child eat sashimi.

You cannot say 子どもを さしみを 食べさせた, but it is usually clear from the context whether the speaker is allowing or making somebody do something.

7 お願いできますか。—いいですよ。おい、山下君、たのむよ。
Yes, could you do that? –Yes. Hey, Yamashita, will you take Mr. Lin to the apartment?

❶ お願いできます is the polite way to say お願いする in its potential form.

❷ よ is a particle used at the end of a sentence for emphasis.

❸ 君 is a suffix on the names of boys or (young) men socially equal or inferior to the speaker.

8 すみません。お世話に なります。
Thank you. I appreciate it.

お世話に なります is a set phrase used when someone is about to do you or the members of your "in-group" a favor. After the favor has been complete お世話に なりました in the polite past form is used. For instance, it is used to mean "thank you for having me" when you stay at over a friend's house, or to thank a doctor or nurse for looking after you.

DRILLS

1. 質問に 答えなさい。
Answer the following questions.

1 不動産屋の 事務所へ だれが やってきましたか。
→ （　　　　　　　）です。

2 林さんは 何を 借りたいと 思って いますか。
→ （　　　　　　　）を 借りたいと 思って います。

3 不動産屋は だれに 案内させましたか。
→ （　　　　　　　）に 案内させました。

2. あなたなら どう しますか。下の 動詞を 使って（　　　）に 言葉を 入れなさい。
What would you do? Fill in the blanks below with the most appropriate verb from the selection below.

1 朝 こどもが「学校へ 行きたくない！」と 言いました。
母親A：学校の 勉強が 大切ですから、ぜったいに（　　　　）せます。
母親B：こどもの 気持ちが 大切ですから、今日は（　　　　）せます。

2 「日本語が 上手に なりたい」と 学生が 言いました。どんな ことを させますか。
先生A：教科書の 文を 何回も 大きい 声で（　　　　）せます。
先生B：教科書の 文を 何回も ノートに（　　　　）せます。

```
書く(to write)      行く(to go)      読む(to read)
走る(to run)        休む(to be absent, to rest)
```

VOCABULARY

- だれ who
- 何(なに) what
- 思(おも)って います is thinking/thinks
- やってきました came over, came along
- 案内(あんない)させました made someone take someone over
- 朝(あさ) [in the] morning
- こども child
- が here, subject particle
- 学校(がっこう) school
- 行(い)きたくない not to want to go
- 言(い)いました said
- 母親(ははおや) mother
- 勉強(べんきょう) study, work
- 大切(たいせつ) important
- から because
- ぜったいに by all means, absolutely
- 気持(きも)ち feeling, thought
- 今日(きょう) today
- 日本語(にほんご) Japanese language
- 上手(じょうず) good at
- ～に なりたい to want to become ～
- 学生(がくせい) student
- どんな what kind of
- こと thing
- させます to make someone do
- 先生(せんせい) teacher
- 教科書(きょうかしょ) textbook
- 文(ぶん) sentence
- 何回(なんかい)も many times
- 大(おお)きい big, loud
- 声(こえ) voice
- で with, by
- ノート notebook

T A S K S

1. だれが だれに 何を させて いるか。
Who is making who do what?

だれが だれに 何を させて いますか。絵に 合った 文を 作って、読んで みましょう。

Using the pictures as a guide, complete the following passage.

1 _____が _____に 手伝わせて います。

お兄さん　　おじいさん

2 _____が 赤ちゃんに ミルクを _____ います。

お母さん　　赤ちゃん

3 お父さんが _____に 本を _____ います。

正夫　　お父さん

4 _____が _____に えさを 食べさせて います。

おばあさん　　犬

5 お姉さんが _____に 手を _____ います。

恵子　　お姉さん

VOCABULARY

- だれ who
- させて います is making [someone] do
- 絵(え) picture
- ～に 合(あ)った matched
- 作(つく)って making
- 読(よ)んで reading
- ～で／(て) みましょう Let's try to ～
- おじいさん grandfather, old man
- お兄(にい)さん older brother
- 手伝(てつだ)う to help, to assist
- お母(かあ)さん mother
- 赤(あか)ちゃん baby
- ミルク milk
- 飲(の)む to drink
- お父(とう)さん father
- 正夫(まさお)、恵子(けいこ) are both given names.
- 本(ほん) book
- おばあさん grandmother, old woman
- 犬(いぬ) dog
- えさ feed, bait
- 食(た)べる to eat
- お姉(ねえ)さん older sister
- 手(て) hand
- 洗(あら)う to wash

2. 台所クイズ　Kitchen quiz

1〜11を ヒントに して、パズルに ことばを 入れ、矢印（↓）の 列に かくされた メッセージを 見つけなさい。

Solve the puzzle by writing in the names of eleven items one might find in the kitchen. The clues on the left-hand side will help you. Read in the direction of the arrow to find the message.

1 これで ケチャップを 作る
2 これで コロッケを 作る
3 この 野菜は ビタミンAが 多い
4 これに ごはんを 入れる
5 これで お湯を わかす
6 これに おかずを のせる
7 この上で 野菜や 魚を 切る
8 むいても むいても 皮だけ
9 これで おかずを にる
10 日本人は この調味料を 一番 よく 使う
11 ポパイは この 野菜を 食べて、強く なる

★ 矢印（↓）の メッセージは？

VOCABULARY

- ヒントに して　using as hints
- パズル　crossword puzzle
- ことば　word, language
- 入(い)れ　inserting
- 矢印(やじるし)　arrow
- 列(れつ)　row, line
- かくされた　hidden
- メッセージ　message
- 見(み)つけなさい　find: an imperative form
- これで　using this
- ケチャップ　ketchup
- 作(つく)る　to make, to prepare
- コロッケ　croquette
- この　this＿
- 野菜(やさい)　vegetable
- ビタミンA　vitamin A
- 多(おお)い　many, much

- 〜に 入(い)れる　to put [somethig] in 〜
- ごはん　steamed rice, meal
- お湯(ゆ)　hot water
- わかす　to boil
- 〜に のせる　to put [something] on 〜
- おかず　side dish
- 上(うえ)　on
- や　and [so on]
- 魚(さかな)　fish
- 切(き)る　to cut
- むいても むいても　no matter how often one peels
- 皮(かわ)　peel, skin
- だけ　only, just
- にる　to cook, to boil
- 日本人(にほんじん)　Japanese [person]
- 調味料(ちょうみりょう)　seasoning, flavoring

- 一番(いちばん)　most, to the greatest degree
- よく　often, frequently
- 使(つか)う　to use
- ポパイ　Popeye
- 食(た)べて　eating
- 強(つよ)く なる　to become strong

NOTES

The 〜ても〜ても construction means "no matter how much/often one does 〜"
For example: わたしは 食(た)べても 食べても 太(ふと)らない。(No matter how much I eat, I don't gain weight.)
むいても むいても 皮(かわ)だけ。(No matter how often [one] peels, only peels [remain].)

12 がんばって ください

Hang in there.

DIALOGUE

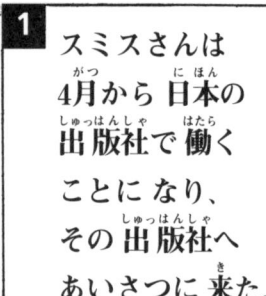

VOCABULARY

- スミスさん　Ms. Smith
- は　as for, speaking of
- 4月　April
- から　from
- 日本　Japan
- の　of
- 出版社　publishing company
- で　at, in, on
- 働く　to work
- ことに なり　being decided to
- その　that
- へ　to
- あいさつ　greeting, self-introduction
- に　for
- 来た　came
- 新しい　new
- 仲間　fellow worker, companion, colleague
- 紹介しよう　to intend to introduce
- 来月　next month
- ここ　here, this place
- 働いて　working
- くれる　to give [a favor]
- だ　is, are, am
- こちら　this [person]
- 係長　chief clerk
- 田中さん　Mr. Tanaka

OBJECTIVES:
Using conditional and passive forms.

- ～で ございます am, is, are
- どうぞ よろしく お願い いたします
  I appreciate your continued support
- です am, is, are
- 分からない not to understand
- こと thing
- あれば if there is
- 何でも anything
- 聞いて ください please ask
- ニッ sound-effect word for smiling face
- もう already
- 長い long, for a long time
- から because
- 何を～ても whatever one does ～
- 聞かれて being asked
- いい good, no problem
- よね isn't it?
- ええ yes
- まあ well
- これから from now on
- いろいろと various [a lot of] things
- 教えて ください please teach
- なかよく やりましょう
  We'll get along well
- がんばって ください Hang in there

CULTURE

Foreigners working for Japanese firms

More non-Japanese are working for Japanese firms all over Japan than ever before. Sometimes a foreign national employed in an overseas branch or subsidiary company is posted to the Tokyo head office of the main company. But more commonly, firms decide to recruit foreign staff on a local-hire basis, often for their intercultural and linguistic skills. Accordingly, such workers usually find themselves placed in either the public relations or international division of a famous and large Japanese corporation. Although they rarely take part in a team that actually generates profit, they serve a useful and important role facilitating easier and more effective international communication. A number of non-Japanese workers can also be seen doing traditionally low-paid and non-skilled jobs, such as laboring on a construction project or washing dishes in the kitchen of a restaurant. Many people from English-speaking countries find work teaching English conversation classes in one of the many private language schools to found in Japan.

PRONUNCIATION

Listen to the tape and repeat. High pitches are marked with ⌈ and low pitches with ⌉. All words appearing in **bold** should be stressed. Note that hyphenated phrases are treated as one word.

1. Sumisu-san-wa shi-gatsu-kara nihon-no shuppansha-de hataraku-koto-ni nari, sono shuppansha-e **aisatsu**-ni kita.

2. **Atarashii** nakama-o shookai-shiyoo.

3. Raigetsu-kara koko-de hataraite kureru **Sumisu-san** da. Kochira-wa kakarichoo-no **Tanaka-san**.

4. **Sumisu**-de gozaimasu. Doozo **yoroshiku** onegai itashimasu.

5. Tanaka-desu. Doozo **yoroshiku**. Wakaranai koto-ga areba, nan-de-mo **kiite** kudasai.

6. Tanaka-san-wa moo nagai-kara, nani-o kikarete-mo **ii-yo-ne**.

   Ee, maa.

7. Kore-kara iroiro-to **oshiete** kudasai.

8. **Nakayoku** yarimashoo. **Ganbatte** kudasai.

NOTES

1 スミスさんは 4月から 日本の 出版社で 働く ことに なり、その 出版社へ あいさつに 来た。
Ms. Smith will begin working for a Japanese publishing company as of April and she has come to the company to introduce herself.

❶ は indicates the topic of the sentence. (See Notes to Module 1.)

❷ から is a particle used here to show a point in time when some action will take place.

❸ の is a particle that here shows the noun after it is modified by the one before it.

❹ で is a particle showing where the action of a verb takes place.

❺ 働く ことに なり The plain form of a verb plus ことに なる indicates an outcome, a decision, or something that has simply happened.

❻ なり is a tense-less bound form of なる that connects the two clauses. なり sounds more formal than the て-form of なる, なって, and its tense is defined by that of the final verb.

❼ へ is a particle that here indicates physical direction and corresponds to "to."

❽ に is a particle which here, preceded by a noun, explains the purpose for the action of the verb that follows.

❾ 来た is the past plain form of 来る.

2 新しい 仲間を 紹介しよう。
I would like to introduce a new colleague.

❶ 新しい is an い-adjective.

❷ を is a particle marking the direct object of a verb.

❸ 紹介しよう The [y]oo form of a verb shows the intention of the speaker to do something; it can also be used in the sense of "let's (do something.)" (See Notes in Module 4.) The more polite way of saying しよう is しましょう.

3 来月から ここで 働いて くれる スミスさんだ。こちらは 係長の 田中さん。
This is Ms. Smith who will start working here next month. This is Mr. Tanaka, our chief clerk.

❶ 働いて is the て-form of 働く.

❷ くれる is used after the て-form of a verb when the speaker is acknowledging that a named person is doing something on behalf of him or the group to which he belongs. (See Module 9 for giving and receiving verbs.)

❸ だ is the plain form of the copula.

❹ こちらは is a polite way to introduce somebody or something, and corresponds to "this is."

4 スミスで ございます。どうぞ よろしく お願い いたします。
My name is Smith. I look forward to working with you.

❶ で ございます is the most polite form of the copula.

❷ Using the more polite いたします rather than します elevates this common phrase to its most formal expression. Similar in register to "nice to meet you," this phrase can be shortened to どうぞ よろしく.

5 田中です。どうぞ よろしく。分からない ことが あれば、何でも 聞いてください。
I am Tanaka. How do you do? If there's anything you don't understand, please ask me.

❶ です is the polite form of the copula.

12 がんばって ください 101

❷ 分からない is the plain negative form of the verb 分かる.
❸ が is a particle showing the subject, here 分からない こと, of a verb.
❹ あれば is the conditional form of the verb ある. This conditional form is made by attaching (r)eba to a verb stem or -kereba to the stem of an い-adjective.

たくさん 食べれば、太ります。(tabe-ru → tabe-reba) If [you] eat a lot [you] will gain weight.
ねだんが 高ければ、わたしは 買いません。(taka-i → taka-kereba) If the price is high, I won't buy it.
わからない ことが あれば、何でも 聞いて ください。(ar-u → ar-eba) (See ⑤ for translation.)

⑥ 田中さんは もう 長いから、何を 聞かれても いいよね。——ええ、まあ。
Mr. Tanaka has worked here for a long time, so he can answer all your questions. –Well, perhaps.

❶ 長い is an い-adjective.
❷ から here is an explanatory conjunction that turns the preceeding statement into a reason for something that follows. (See Notes to Module 10.)
❸ 聞かれて is the て-form of the passive 聞かれる from the verb 聞く.

The passive:
The passive verb basically means "to be affected by an action or state," and is formed by adding (r)are-ru [plain] /masu [polite] to the stem of the verb, whether it is transitive or intransitive. Someone/something that affects someone/something, i.e., an agent, is marked with に in the passive sentence. (Note that the direct objects, i.e. 足を and 何を below, remain as they are in the passive sentence.)

（わたしは） 子どもに 泣かれた。(nak-u → nak-are-ta) [I] was affected by my child crying.
子どもが 先生に ほめられた。(home-ru → home-rare-ta) [My] child was praised by the teacher.
山口さんは 犬に 足を かまれた。(kam-u → kam-are-ta) Mr. Yamaguchi's leg was bitten by a dog.
田中さんは もう 長いから、何を 聞かれても いいよね。(kik-u → kik-are-te-mo) (See above.)

❹ 〜ても いい it is OK (permitted) that 〜 .
❺ よ is a particle used here for emphasis.
❻ ね is used to confirm the preceeding statement for the speaker.
❼ ええ is a more informal way of saying はい.
❽ まあ indicates hesitation on the speaker's part.

⑦ これから いろいろと 教えて ください。
I would appreciate your help.

❶ これから corresponds to the English "from now on."
❷ 教えて ください is the polite request form for the verb 教える.

⑧ なかよく やりましょう。がんばって ください。
I think we will work well together. Hang in there.

❶ やりましょう is the polite form of やろう, which employs the [y]oo form to indicate inclination to do something. (See Notes to Module 4.)
❷ がんばって ください is the polite request form of がんばる. Although its meaning is quite different, it is often used where an English-speaker would say "Good Luck!"

DRILLS

1. 質問に 答えなさい。
Answer the following questions.

1　スミスさんは いつから どこで 働く ことに なりましたか。
　→ (　　　　)から (　　　　)で 働く ことに なりました。

2　スミスさんは 出版社へ 何を しに 来ましたか。
　→ (　　　　)を しに 来ました。

3　係長は だれですか。
　→ (　　　　)です。

4　何を 聞かれても いい 人は だれですか。
　→ (　　　　)です。

2. 動詞の 形を 変えて、文を 完成させなさい。
Complete the following sentences by transforming the plain form of the verb into its conditional.

1　あなたが (行く→　　　　)ば、わたしも 行きます。
2　お金が (ある→　　　　)ば、海外旅行を したいです。
3　牛肉を たくさん (食べる→　　　　)ば、太ります。
4　ねだんが (高い→　　　　)ば、わたしは 買いません。
5　雨が (降らない→　　　　)ば、植物は 育ちません。
6　今日 (暑くない→　　　　)ば、冷房を つけないで ください。
7　運動を (する→　　　　)ば、健康に なります。

VOCABULARY

- いつ　when
- どこ　where
- ことに なりました　was decided
- か　question particle
- しに　in order to do
- 来(き)ました　came
- だれ　who
- 人(ひと)　person
- あなた　you
- 行(い)く　to go
- わたし　I
- も　also
- 行(い)きます　to go
- お金(かね)　money
- ある　to have, to exist
- 海外旅行(かいがいりょこう)　overseas travel
- したい　to want to do
- 牛肉(ぎゅうにく)　beef
- たくさん　much, many
- 食(た)べる　to eat
- 太(ふと)ります　to gain weight
- ねだん　price
- 高(たか)い　high
- 買(か)いません　not to buy
- 雨(あめ)　rain
- 降(ふ)らない　not to fall, not to rain
- 植物(しょくぶつ)　plant
- 育(そだ)ちません　not to grow
- 今日(きょう)　today
- 暑(あつ)くない　not hot
- 冷房(れいぼう)　air conditioning
- つけないで ください　Please don't turn on
- 運動(うんどう)　physical exercises
- する　to do
- 健康(けんこう)に なります　to become healthy

TASKS

1. だれが だれに どう されたか？
   What is done to whom by whom?

下の 絵を 見て、次の 文を 完成させなさい。

Using the picture as an aid, complete the following sentences.

(例) わたしと 妹は 父に おみやげを 頼んだ。→ 父は わたしと 妹に おみやげを 頼まれた。

1 _____は 兄に 文句を 言った。→ _____は 父に _____。
2 兄は 田中さんを 尊敬して いる。→ _____は _____に 尊敬されて いる。
3 田中さんは _____の 写真を 撮った。→ 秋山先生は _____に _____。
4 秋山先生は _____を _____。→ 学生は _____に しかられた。
5 学生は _____を 読んだ。→ わたしと 妹は _____に 手紙を _____。

父   わたしと妹   学生

兄   田口さん   秋山先生

VOCABULARY

- 下(した) below
- 絵(え) picture, drawing
- 見(み)て looking at
- 次(つぎ) next, following
- 文(ぶん) sentence
- 完成(かんせい)させなさい complete: an imperative form
- 例(れい) example
- と and
- 妹(いもうと) [my] younger sister
- 父(ちち) [my] father
- おみやげ souvenir, present
- 頼(たの)んだ asked [a favor]
- 頼(たの)まれた was asked [a favor]
- 兄(あに) [my] older brother
- に to
- 文句(もんく) complaint, objection
- 言(い)った said
- 尊敬(そんけい)して いる is respecting, to respect
- 尊敬(そんけい)されて いる is respected
- 写真(しゃしん) photo, picture
- 撮(と)った took [a photo]
- 秋山先生(あきやませんせい) Professor Akiyama
- 学生(がくせい) student
- しかられた was scolded
- 読(よ)んだ read
- 手紙(てがみ) letter

2. 診断テスト：あなたの 日本語は だいじょうぶ？
Evaluation test: Is your Japanese OK?

次の 問に 答えなさい。それぞれ 1点です。得点に よって、あなたの 日本語を 診断します。

Answer the following questions. One point will be given to each correct answer, and your Japanese will be evaluated based on your total points.

問1 （　）の 中の 動詞を 正しい 形に 変えなさい。

Change the verbs in parentheses into appropriate forms.

a　ここは「禁煙」ですから、たばこは（すう）で ください。（→ Module 3）

b　スミスさんは 映画の 切符を（もらう）ので、あした（見る）に 行く つもりです。
　　（→ Module 10）

c　わたしは 日本語の 先生に（なる）たいです。（→ Module 4）

d　キムさんは 鈴木先生に 本を（かす）て もらいました。（→ Module 9）

e　田中さんは 来年 ヨーロッパへ（行く）と 思って います。（→ Module 4）

f　わたしは 毎日 赤ちゃんに ミルクを（飲む）せます。（→ Module 11）

g　山口さんは 犬に 足を（かむ）れました。（→ Module 12）

h　林さんは 音楽を（聞く）ながら 勉強します。（→ Module 2）

VOCABULARY

- 次（つぎ）　next, following
- 問（とい）　question
- 〜に 答（こた）えなさい
　answer 〜 : an imperative form
- それぞれ　each
- 1点（いってん）　one point
- 得点（とくてん）　the points made
- 〜に よって
　based on 〜 , according to 〜
- あなたの　your
- 日本語（にほんご）
　the Japanese language
- 診断（しんだん）します
　to evaluate, to examine
- 禁煙（きんえん）　no smoking
- です　is, are, am
- から　because
- たばこ　tobacco, cigarette
- すう　to smoke
- 映画（えいが）　movie
- 切符（きっぷ）　ticket
- もらう　to receive
- ので　because
- あした　tomorrow
- 見（み）る　to watch, to see
- つもり　intention
- 日本語（にほんご）
　the Japanese language
- なる　to become
- たい　to want to
- キムさん　Ms. Kim
- 鈴木先生（すずきせんせい）
　Professor Suzuki
- 本（ほん）　book
- かす　to lend
- もらいました　received (a favor)
- 来年（らいねん）　next year
- ヨーロッパ　Europe
- と 思って います
　is thinking that, think that
- 毎日（まいにち）　everyday
- 赤（あか）ちゃん　baby
- ミルク　milk
- 飲（の）む　to drink
- 山口（やまぐち）さん
　Mr./Ms. Yamaguchi
- 犬（いぬ）　dog
- 足（あし）　leg
- かむ　to bite
- 林（りん）さん　Mr. Lin
- 音楽（おんがく）　music
- 聞（き）く　to listen
- 勉強（べんきょう）します　to study

問2 次の 文の 下線部分の 間違いを 訂正しなさい。
Correct the mistake, which is underlined, in each sentence.

a 林さんは 毎週 一回 中国の <u>お母さんを</u> 電話を かけます。(→ Module 6)
b スミスさんは もう 少しで 終電車に <u>乗り遅れた</u> ところでした。(→ Module 8)
c ねだんが <u>安ければ</u> 買います。(→ Module 12)
d パリへ <u>行きます</u> 前に ロンドンへ 行きました。(→ Module 1)
e 橋で <u>渡って</u> もう 少し 行くと、病院が あります。(→ Module 2, Module 8)
f 鈴木先生は 毎晩 ビールを <u>お飲みします</u>。(→ Module 7)

●あなたの 得点は 何点でしたか。●

1~6点：残念ですが、日本で 一人で 旅行するのは 無理です。この 本を 使って、もう 一度 勉強して ください。

7~12点：もう 少し 日本語の 練習が 必要です。東京や 京都へ 旅行して、日本語を 使って みましょう。

13~15点：よく 勉強しましたね。一人で 北海道でも 九州でも 自由に 旅行できます。

VOCABULARY

- 毎週(まいしゅう) every week
- 一回(いっかい) once
- 中国(ちゅうごく) China
- お母(かあ)さん (someone's) mother
- 電話(でんわ)を かけます to make a phone call
- もう 少(すこ)しで by a little more
- 終電車(しゅうでんしゃ) last train
- 乗(の)り遅(おく)れた missed (the train)
- ところでした was about to
- ねだん price
- 安(やす)い cheap
- 買(か)います to buy
- パリ Paris
- へ to
- 前(まえ)に before
- ロンドン London
- 行(い)きました went
- 橋(はし) bridge
- 渡(わた)って crossing
- 行(い)くと if (you) go
- 病院(びょういん) hospital
- あります there is, to exist
- 毎晩(まいばん) every night
- ビール beer
- 飲(の)みます to drink
- あなたの your
- 何点(なんてん) how many points
- でした was, were
- 残念(ざんねん) regrettable
- が but
- 日本(にほん)で in Japan
- 一人(ひとり)で by oneself, alone
- 旅行(りょこう)するの traveling, to travel
- 無理(むり) impossible
- この this
- 使(つか)って using
- もう 一度(いちど) one more time
- 勉強(べんきょう)して ください please study
- 練習(れんしゅう) practice
- 必要(ひつよう) necessary
- 東京(とうきょう)や 京都(きょうと) Tokyo, Kyoto, (and other places)
- 旅行(りょこう)して traveling
- 使(つか)って みましょう let's try using
- よく well
- 勉強(べんきょう)しました studied
- 北海道(ほっかいどう)でも even in Hokkaido
- 九州(きゅうしゅう) Kyushu
- 自由(じゆう)に freely
- 旅行(りょこう)できます can travel

ANSWERS

DRILLS

module 1 — P15

1 1.スミスさん 2.林さん 3.林さん 4.スミスさん

2 a.13 b.10 c.7 d.4 e.15 f.1 g.12 h.9 i.6 j.3 k.11 l.2 m.14 n.5 o.8

module 2 — P23

1 1.スミスさん 2.国際免許証 3.郵便局か銀行

2 1.かかないで 2.きいて 3.はなして 4.かさないで 5.むすばないで 6.あそんで 7.うって 8.のらないで 9.たべないで 10.あけて 11.しないで 12.いって 13.およがないで 14.いそいで 15.まって 16.たたないで 17.よまないで 18.のんで 19.かって 20.うたわないで 21.みないで 22.かりて 23.きて

module 3 — P31

1 1.スミスさん 2.病院 3.38度5分 4.ちゅうしゃ、(お)薬

module 4 — P39

1 1.京都 2.10, 4 3.5140円 4.自由席

2 1.休んだ 2.いたかった 3.結婚している 4.行った 5.借りたい 6.思っている

module 5 — P47

1 1.林さん 2.ろばた焼き 3.肉 4.かれい

2 1.多い 2.暑い 3.低い 4.新しい 5.遅い 6.大きい 7.長い

module 6 — P55

1 1.パテルさん、9月10日 2.佐藤さん 3.8月26日 4.土曜日

2 1.しよう 2.した 3.そう 4.思う 5.ある 6.じょうずだ 7.聞き

module 7 — P63

1 1.デパート 2.佐藤さん or 佐藤夫人 3.のういっけつ

2 1.お手紙 2.おなりになる or なられる 3.お忙しい 4.お元気 5.お好きな 6.お酒 7.お飲みになる or 飲まれる 8.ごらんになる or 見られる

module 8 — P71

1 1.スミスさん 2.タクシー 3.150 4.雑誌

2 1.起きた 2.飲んでいる 3.乗り遅れる

module 9　　　P79

1 1.佐藤さん　2.おもち　3.フルーツケーキ

2 1.あげました　2.さしあげました　3.くださいました　4.もらいました
　5.いただきました

module 10　　　P87

1 1.鈴木先生　2.孫の愛子ちゃん　3.明治神宮で撮った写真　4.鈴木先生

2 1.ので is preferable　2.から is preferable　3.から

module 11　　　P95

1 1.林さん　2.今朝見たアパート　3.山下君

2 1.行か、休ま　2.読ま、書か

module 12　　　P103

1 1.4月、日本の出版社　2.あいさつ　3.田中さん　4.田中さん

2 1.行け　2.あれ　3.食べれ　4.高けれ　5.降らなけれ　6.暑くなけれ　7.すれ

TASKS

module 1　　　P16~17

1 1.プール　2.やまとレストラン　3.ホテルあさだ　4.本屋　5.喫茶店　6.公園

2 C

module 2　　　P24~25

1 A.2　B.2　C.2　D.3　E.1

2 1.8　2.7　3.5　4.6　5.3

module 3　　　P33

1 1.山下さん　2.上田さん　3.岡島さん　4.中島さん

module 4　　　P40~41

1 ハンカチ7、音楽テープ3、本4、くつした1

　1.にそく　2.きゅうさつ　3.ななまい　4.じっぽん　5.にまい　6.さんぼん
　7.ごそく　8.はっさつ　9.よんさつ　10.さんぞく　11.ごほん　12.よんまい
　13.ななまい　14.ろっぽん　15.いっそく　16.いっさつ

2 1.スーザンさん　2.のぼるさんとカールさん　3.ホセさんの切符

module 5　　　P48~49

1 1.ゆみさん　2.信子さん　3.まさみさん　4.ゆみさん　5.8匹

2 1.28　2.27　3.30　4.29　5.50,000　6.0　7.30,000　8.60,000　9.1　10.0　11.2　12.3

module 6　P56~57

1 B.キム C.王(おう) D.パテル E.スミス F.林(りん)

2 B

module 7　P64~65

1 1.f 2.g 3.c 4.a 5.e 6.b 7.d

2 B E C F A G D

module 8　P72~73

1 a.あそこ b.あの c.それ d.これ e.ここ f.この g.これ h.これ i.あれ j.それ k.その

2 a.3 b.4 c.1 d.2 e.6 f.7 g.10 h.5 i.9 j.8

module 9　P80~81

1 1.もらった、あげました 2.くれませんか、もらいました 3.もらって、あげました、あげました 4.くれませんか

2 グラフ3

module 10　P88~89

1 1.h 2.a 3.f 4.b 5.d 6.e 7.g 8.j

2 1.インディラとエドワード 2.ゴルフ場 3.インディラとエドワード 4.2時(じ)半(はん)から4時ごろ 5.エドワードとあきら 6.6時15分(ふん)から8時ごろ

module 11　P96~97

1 1.おじいさん、お兄(にい)さん 2.お母(かあ)さん、飲(の)ませて 3.正夫(まさお)、読(よ)ませて 4.おばあさん、犬(いぬ) 5.恵子(けいこ)、洗(あら)わせて

2 1.トマト tomato 2.じゃがいも potato 3.にんじん carrot 4.ちゃわん bowl 5.やかん kettle 6.さら plate 7.まないた chopping board 8.たまねぎ onion 9.なべ pan 10.しょうゆ soy sauce 11.ほうれんそう spinach

メッセージ：まいにちやさいをたべよう

module 12　P104~106

1 1.父(ちち)、兄(あに)、文句(もんく)を言(い)われた 2.田中(たなか)さん、兄(あに) 3.秋山(あきやま)先生(せんせい)、田中さん、写真(しゃしん)を撮(と)られた 4.学生(がくせい)、しかった、秋山先生 5.私(わたし)と妹(いもうと)の手紙(てがみ)、学生、読(よ)まれた

2 問1 a.すわない b.もらった、見(み) c.なり d.かし e.行(い)こう f.飲(の)ま g.かま h.聞(き)き

問2 a.お母(かあ)さんに b.乗(の)り遅(おく)れる c.安(やす)ければ d.行(い)く e.橋(はし)を f.お飲(の)みになります

GRAMMAR INDEX

(1) particles

で reason, cause ········· 21, 62
で instrument ········· 30, 37
で location ········· 22, 54, 61, 70, 85, 101
へ direction 14, 29, 37, 45, 53, 69, 78, 93, 101
が subject
········· 13, 21, 29, 38, 53, 61, 71, 78, 85, 102
が conjunction ········· 32, 37, 53, 54, 62, 78, 93
が direct object ········· 45
か "or" ········· 22, 54
から "from" ········· 14, 101
から conjunction ········· 78, 85, 86, 87, 102
まで "as far as, until" ········· 69
も "also" ········· 30, 46, 62, 78, 93
に inderect object ········· 13
に time ········· 14, 86, 89
に location ········· 21
に purpose ········· 37, 46, 48, 62, 86, 88, 101
に direction ········· 53, 69
に agent ········· 77, 85, 94
の "of" ········· 21, 37, 45, 53, 69, 70, 85, 93, 101
を direct object
········· 13, 21, 37, 45, 53, 63, 69, 77, 85, 93, 101
を location ········· 24, 25, 69
を departing place ········· 33, 73
と condition ········· 25, 73
と quotaton ········· 37, 53, 81, 86, 93
と "and" ········· 38, 45, 93
と co-actor ········· 80
は topic
········· 13, 21, 29, 37, 45, 53, 69, 85, 93, 101

(2) sentence-final particles

か question ········· 14, 29, 37, 53, 62, 86
かな "wonder" ········· 54, 77
かしら "wonder" ········· 77
な confirmation ········· 46, 81
ね confirmation
········· 22, 30, 37, 46, 54, 61, 69, 77, 93, 102
のよ emphasis ········· 57, 81

わ assertion 45, 57, 81
よ emphasis 22, 70, 78, 94
よね confirmation 102

(3) ある／あります or いる／います
to describe the whereabouts of something /
someone 21, 53, 56, 73

(4) causative form 94, 95, 96

(5) comparative sentence 45, 47, 48, 49, 54, 81

(6) copulas
だ 21, 101
だった 62
です 13, 22, 37, 69, 77, 86, 93, 101
でした 62

(7) counters 40, 48, 49, 71, 73

(8) でございます the most polite copula
.... 53, 61, 101

(9) でしょう confirmation 94

(10) でしょう "will probably be" 17, 24, 64

(11) giving and receiving verbs
.... 77, 78, 79; 80, 81, 85, 93, 101

(12) honorific form 53, 61, 62, 63

(13) humble form 86, 93

(14) い-adjective
.... 29, 30, 31, 32, 47, 54, 77, 78, 94, 101

(15) かもしれません might 87

(16) これ（この）、それ（その）、あれ（あの）
どれ（どの） demonstratives 72, 73, 78

(17) ことにする to decide to do something
.... 69, 77

(18) ことになる
to be decided to do something 101

(19) ませんか
to invite someone to do something ... 80, 86

(20) ました past tense 14

(21) ましょう or [y]oo form to indicate one's
intention
ましょう 30, 101, 102
[y]oo 37, 46, 53, 54, 55, 86, 101

(22) な-adjective 29, 45, 62, 85

(23) ながら "while doing ～" 22

(24) なさい imperative form
.... 16, 33, 49, 72, 80, 88, 89, 97, 104, 105

(25) のだ／のです to make a sentence more
colloquial, emphatic, and explanatory
.... 37, 39, 46, 54, 62, 78, 93

(26) ので vs. から conjunction
ので 85, 87
から 78, 85, 86, 87, 102

(27) お or ご honorific prefix
.... 14, 61, 62, 63, 70, 78

(28) お polite prefix 30, 46, 70

(29) passive form 102, 104

(30) plain vs. polite form 13

(31) potential form 30, 33, 49, 87, 94

(32) そうだ／そうです to express hearsay
.... 54, 55

(33) subordinate clause 17, 22

(34) superlative sentence 41, 46, 47, 48, 81

(35) たい form to express one's wish or desire
.... 37, 55, 78, 93

(36) ている／います to indicate a continuing
action or state 37, 53, 56, 73, 78, 94

(37) て／で ください polite request
.... 21, 24, 30, 62, 69, 102

(38) て／で form to connect clauses
.... 21-22, 29, 30, 32, 38, 45, 69, 86, 89

(39) ても いい permission 102

(40) ～ても ～ても "no matter how much/often
one does ～" 97

(41) と, (r)eba, ければ conditionals
と 25, 73
(r)eba, ければ 102, 103

(42) ところ to describe a time or state
.... 70, 71, 78, 86

(43) verbal bound form to connect clauses
.... 21-22, 89, 101